HOW WIT ...RDS

In recent decades, the contested areas of English usage have grown both larger and more numerous. English speakers argue about whether we should say *man* or *humanity*, *fisher* or *fisherman*; whether we ought to speak of people as being *disabled*, or *challenged*, or *differently abled*; whether it is acceptable to say *that's so gay*. More generally, we ask, can we use language in ways that avoid giving expression to prejudices embedded within it? Can the words we use help us point a way towards a better world? Can we ask such questions with appropriate seriousness while remaining open-minded—and while retaining our sense of humor? To all these questions this concise and user-friendly guide answers yes, while offering clear-headed discussions of many of the key issues.

Don LePan is co-author of *The Broadview Guide to Writing* (sixth edition 2017) and of *The Broadview Pocket Glossary of Literary Terms* (2014); his second novel, *Rising Stories*, was published in 2015. **Laura Buzzard** is co-author of *The Broadview Pocket Glossary of Literary Terms* (2014) and co-editor of *The Broadview Anthology of Expository Prose* (third edition 2016), and *Science and Society: An Anthology for Readers and Writers* (2014). **Maureen Okun** is Professor of English and of Liberal Studies at Vancouver Island University; she has edited *Sir Thomas Malory's Le Morte Darthur: Selections* (2014) and is co-author of *The Broadview Guide to Writing* (sixth edition 2017) and *The Broadview Pocket Guide to Citation and Documentation* (second edition 2016).

HOW TO BE GOOD WITH WORDS

Don LePan, Laura Buzzard, and
Maureen Okun

broadview press

BROADVIEW PRESS — www.broadviewpress.com
Peterborough, Ontario, Canada

Founded in 1985, Broadview Press remains a wholly independent publishing
house. Broadview's focus is on academic publishing; our titles are accessible to
university and college students as well as scholars and general readers. With
over 600 titles in print, Broadview has become a leading international publisher
in the humanities, with world-wide distribution. Broadview is committed to
environmentally responsible publishing and fair business practices.

The interior of this book is printed on 100% recycled paper.

Library and Archives Canada Cataloguing in Publication

LePan, Don, 1954–, author
    How to be good with words / Don LePan, Laura Buzzard, and Maureen Okun.

Includes bibliographical references and index.
ISBN 978-1-55481-325-4 (softcover)

        1. English language—Usage. I. Buzzard, Laura, author II. Okun, Maureen,
1961–, author III. Title.

PE1460.L46 2017   428   C2017-900069-1

Broadview Press handles its own distribution in North America
PO Box 1243, Peterborough, Ontario K9J 7H5, Canada
555 Riverwalk Parkway, Tonawanda, NY 14150, USA
Tel: (705) 743-8990; Fax: (705) 743-8353
email: customerservice@broadviewpress.com

Distribution is handled by Eurospan Group in the UK, Europe, Central Asia,
Middle East, Africa, India, Southeast Asia, Central America, South America, and
the Caribbean. Distribution is handled by Footprint Books in Australia and New
Zealand.

Broadview Press acknowledges the financial support
of the Government of Canada through the Canada
Book Fund for our publishing activities.

Book design and typeset by Alexandria Stuart
Cover design by Lisa Brawn

PRINTED IN CANADA

CONTENTS

contents

contents

contents

HOW TO USE THIS BOOK

One way in which a book such as this one may be used is simply as a reference guide by anyone wishing, for example, to find the best non-sexist alternative to *caveman* or *freshman*, or the most appropriate term to use for a violent extremist of a particular stripe. Our hope, though, is that the book will be valued for more than simply reference—that it may be useful in a wide range of undergraduate courses as a prompt to informed discussion of issues related to the ethical use of language. Many Introductory Writing and Introductory Communications instructors (as well as instructors in a variety of more advanced courses on gender, on race, and so on) already discuss these matters with their students either on an occasional basis or in a focused way, as one component of a full-semester course. We've heard from a number of those academics that classroom discussions on such topics can be lively and productive. Until now, however, there has not been any volume devoted to a consideration of these issues that was intended for an undergraduate audience; this book is intended to fill that gap.

The discussions in these pages are designed, first of all, to provide background on why some particular usages may be preferred over others—to give students a sense of the reasoning involved, and of the history of various words and phrases. We try as well to convey clearly that history is still happening, and that on many issues there is a good deal of room for lively discussion—and reasonable disagreement—as to what words or phrases are best in particular circumstances. Throughout the body of the book we periodically pose questions that are designed to provoke focused discussion of the issues.

Also of interest—and of real relevance to a variety of undergraduate courses—are questions of etymology and patterns of use of particular words and expressions; discussing those sorts of background matters in a dispassionate way can provide a good balance to the sometimes-impassioned discussions that are likely to arise over issues of gender and language, race and language, and so on. Many of the suggestions for discussion that appear at the end of each chapter are designed to encourage dispassionate exploration of the former sort.

Some of the suggestions for discussion make use of the Google Ngram Viewer (https://books.google.com/ngrams), which searches the vast corpus of published works that Google has scanned (currently covering the period 1500–2008) for frequency of use. Once you have accessed the viewer, simply enter the term(s) you wish to check, separated by commas, then click "Search," and an "Ngram" chart will show you the historical changes in the frequency with which the term(s) have been used. The default historical graph provided will cover the period 1800–2000, but you can adjust the dates at the top left; currently the earliest and latest dates for which information is provided are 1500 and 2008, respectively.

Acknowledgments

The authors are grateful to the many academics who have offered comments and suggestions. In this connection we would particularly like to acknowledge the following: Jake Ackeral; Linda Coleman, University of Maryland; Margery Fee, University of British Columbia; Corey Frost, New Jersey City University; Steve Guthrie, Agnes Scott College; David Leonard, Washington State University; Anahid Nersessian, University of California, Los Angeles; Jocelyn Sakal Froese, Wilfrid Laurier University; Alexandria Stuart, Broadview Press; Karen Weingarten, Queens College, CUNY; Audrey Yap, University of Victoria; Liam Young, University of Alberta.

how to use
this book

INTRODUCTION

For authors of writing guides, the question of how to approach issues such as sexist language and cultural bias has often been a vexed one. The most popular writing handbook (*A Writer's Reference*, by Diana Hacker and Nancy Sommers, 8e, 2016), includes a section entitled "Avoid sexist language," followed by a section entitled "Revise language that may offend groups of people." The first of these headings is surely unproblematic (we will come in a moment to the issue of gender and language). But what of the second? Should we really avoid all language that "may offend groups of people"? If so, George Orwell and Simone de Beauvoir and Martin Luther King Jr. and Nelson Mandela should certainly not have spoken out as plainly as they did. If so, we should never use a phrase such as "the cruelties of factory farming," for it is surely offensive to most managers of what they would prefer to call "intensive farming operations" or "concentrated animal feeding operations." If so, we would have to be quite inventive in referring to the bitumen extraction industry in northern Alberta, since one group is offended if the phrase "tar sands" is used, while an equally large group is offended if the alternative term, "oil sands," is used. The point about non-sexist language and culturally sensitive language, then, is not that you should never be willing to use language that might offend. It is that you should try never to use language that stereotypes particular groups, or that presumes other groups to be inferior.

Another leading writing handbook—Andrea Lunsford's *The Everyday Writer* (5e, 2012) introduces this topic by referencing the so-called "golden rule"—*Do unto others as you would have them do unto you*—a Christian concept that has parallels in numerous other religions. "The golden rule of language," writes Lunsford, "might be 'Speak to others the way you want them to speak to you.'" But surely this is precisely what we should *not* always do if we are truly to be considerate of others. A young person in the habit of using crude language might well prefer others to respond to him in the same way—to tell him that anything he has accomplished is "f—ing fantastic," for example. But in most cases it would be both inconsiderate and unwise of him to use the same language to his grandparents. Another young person might be pleased to hear from a friend that she looks really sexy in her new outfit. But it would in most cases be both inconsiderate and unwise of her to speak in the same way to a young woman wearing a nun's habit. The point, then, is not that we should do or say to others exactly what we would like them to do or say to us, but that we should be considerate of them, just as we would want them to be considerate to us. Rather than presuming others to be like us, we should try to think of how they might like to be treated, and of how that in many cases might be different from our own preferences.

This book has its origin in a section of *The Broadview Guide to Writing* that first appeared under the title "Bias-Free Language." That was a title we adopted in large part to get away from negatively focused headings such as "sexist language" or "biased language," or "the language of prejudice." But "bias-free" is a term that can perhaps too easily take on a self-congratulatory ring. We should surely all keep trying to find and use bias-free language, but we should also always try to remember that none of us will ever be entirely free of bias or prejudice—and that the struggle against it is not only an ongoing one in society as a whole, but also a lifelong one within each one of us.

Most writing guides and handbooks inform the reader that certain usages "are considered" inappropriate (and provide a short list), but do not devote much space to explaining why. Our intent in this book is both to provide wider coverage of inappropriate usages than is available in a typical sort of writing guide, and to go into greater detail as to why they are considered inappropriate. In some cases, where there really is no consensus about what usage is best, we have chosen not to gloss over these uncertainties but to outline the debate so that writers using this guide can choose an informed position for themselves. We have also included at the end of each chapter a selection of cases for consideration, drawing attention to controversies and open questions regarding the ethical use of language; in a few of these, where even the authors of this book did not agree, we have presented contrasting viewpoints. We include substantial discussions of issues relating to gender, race, class, religion, sexual orientation, disability, non-human animals, and political controversy—but of course it would be impossible to cover every ethical consideration that might come up in writing. Our hope is that this guide will not just offer concrete advice about particular words and phrasings, but also demonstrate an approach to ethical writing that can be useful in all sorts of contexts.

Some General Principles

Relatively few people in North American society are overtly bigoted in the style that was routine a little over a century ago—though any visit to a news website's comments section

introduction

will demonstrate how far there is still to go. But the context in which such language is used has changed; well into the twentieth century it was still common to hear in respectable North American society language that was overtly sexist, or racist, or anti-Jewish, or anti-Catholic, or anti-Polish, or anti-Italian, or contemptuous of "the lower classes." The sorts of crude slur that were routine then have very largely disappeared from accepted usage, but many of the old prejudices persist in subtler forms, and not a few new ones have taken root as well. If they are not always visible or audible in polite company, they nevertheless can have devastating effects. Experiments in which large numbers of identical resumes are sent out, for example, indicate that a person with an African American-sounding name is far less likely to be granted an interview than is a person with a white American-sounding name and exactly the same credentials.[1] Similarly, in France someone with a Muslim-sounding name is vastly less likely to be considered for a job than someone with a traditional French name.[2] Similar studies have found that a woman is far less likely to be considered for a science-related position at Yale University than is a man with identical credentials.[3]

introduction

---

1   See, for example, Marianne Bertrand and Sendhil Mullainathan, "Are Emily and Greg More Employable than Lakisha and Jamal? A Field Experiment on Labor Market Discrimination," NBER Working Paper No. 9873, July 2003. Bertrand and Mullainathan found that white job applicants are 50 percent more likely to receive an interview than African American ones.

2   See Claire L. Adida, David D. Laitin, and Marie-Anne Valfort, "Identifying Barriers to Muslim Integration in France," *PNAS* vol. 107, no. 52, 28 December 2010. Laitin et al. found that in France a Muslim candidate is two and a half times less likely to be interviewed than a Christian one.

3   See Corinne A. Moss-Racusin et al., "Science Faculty's Subtle Biases Favor Male Students," *PNAS* vol. 109, no. 41, 9 October 2012. Moss-Racusin et al. also found that women were offered lower starting salaries than men with the same credentials.

Often, of course, prejudices are held silently—and often they are held in our subconscious rather than our conscious mind. Often, too, a style that is considerate to others is not simply a matter of avoiding prejudiced words. It is always good to think about the first or third person pronouns one is using, and who they may include or exclude. In some cases it may be better to repeat a noun than to replace it with a pronoun. Consider these examples in which writers discuss a group they do not belong to, but which members of the audience they are addressing may well be a part of:

worth checking The twentieth century brought a revolution in the roles that women play in North American society; in 1900 they still were not allowed to vote in any North American jurisdiction.

[If the writer is male and addressing an audience of both women and men, it is more inclusive to avoid using the third person "they."]

revised The twentieth century brought a revolution in the roles that women play in North American society; in 1900 women still were not allowed to vote in any North American jurisdiction.

or The twentieth century brought a revolution in gender roles in North American society; in 1900 women still were not allowed to vote in any North American jurisdiction.

worth checking In the late twentieth and early twenty-first centuries several rulings by the Supreme

introduction

Court altered the landscape considerably where Canada's Aboriginal peoples are concerned. They now have much greater leverage when it comes to natural resource issues than they did before the Court's Delgamuukw and Tsilhqot'in decisions.

[If the writer is not Aboriginal and is addressing an Aboriginal audience or an audience that could include both Aboriginal and non-Aboriginal people, it is more inclusive to avoid using the third-person "they" and "them."]

revised In the late twentieth and early twenty-first centuries several rulings by the Supreme Court altered the landscape considerably where Canada's Aboriginal peoples are concerned. First Peoples now have much greater leverage when it comes to natural resource issues than was the case before the Court's Delgamuukw and Tsilhqot'in decisions.

worth checking I would like to conclude my remarks with a prayer that has meant a great deal to me. We all know how God can bring light into our lives; certainly He has done so for me.

[This is appropriate if the speaker is addressing a crowd that she knows is entirely made up of fellow believers— but inappropriate if the speaker is addressing a mixed crowd of believers, agnostics, and atheists.]

revised I would like to conclude my remarks with a prayer that has meant a great deal to me.

> Many of you may have experienced the feeling of God bringing light into your life; certainly He has done that for me.
>
> [This is appropriate if the speaker is addressing a mixed crowd of believers, agnostics, and atheists.]

A related issue often arises in writing dealing with political and cultural issues. It is all too easy to slip into language that presumes the norm in one's own area to be the norm throughout the entire country, or the norm in one's own society to be the norm worldwide. In such situations it is worth taking the time to find wording that is more precise.

worth checking In the world we live in today, most people learn to drive before they reach their late twenties.

[This is no doubt true in North America and much of Europe—but it is certainly not true of "most people" in India, or Nigeria, or Papua New Guinea. Overall, far fewer than half the world's population learn to drive at any age.]

revised In the United States and Canada today, most people learn to drive before they reach their late twenties.

Another unconsciously biased habit to avoid is the use of unnecessary racial or religious identifiers. Mentioning a person's gender, race, religion, or sexual orientation in connection with occupation is a common habit, but one that reinforces stereotypes as to what sort of person one would naturally expect to be a lawyer or a doctor or a nurse. Unless race or gender or religion is in some way relevant to the conversation, it is inappropriate to refer to someone as a male nurse, or a Jewish doctor, or a Native lawyer. Here's an example from the 17 October 2012 issue of *The Globe and Mail*: "A female Canadian border guard was shot at one of the country's busiest crossings Tuesday." Is there any reason to foreground the sex of the border guard in this way? If the guard had been a man, the writer would surely not have written "A male Canadian border guard was...." Whereas using gender-neutral terms helps to reinforce our acceptance of the idea that occupations are not inherently male or female, terms such as "female border guard" (or "female electrician," or "male nurse," or "woman doctor") work in the opposite direction, reinforcing old stereotypes.

Similarly, the more we foreground a person's race when it is *not* a characteristic relevant to the discussion, the more we encourage people to emphasize race rather than focusing on other human attributes.

worth checking I was given a ticket for speeding last week; a Black police officer pulled me over just after I'd crossed the Port Mann bridge. So I had to pay the bridge toll and an eighty dollar fine!

revised I was given a ticket for speeding last week; a police officer pulled me over just after I'd crossed the Port Mann bridge. So I had to pay the bridge toll and an eighty dollar fine!

worth checking I've heard that Professor Andover's course in Canadian literature is very interesting.

> She's of Asian background from the look
> of her; she just joined the department this
> year. Apparently she's an expert on Leon-
> ard Cohen and the connections between
> literature and music.

[It may not be immediately apparent to some readers
that there is anything odd or problematic about this
example. Substitute "She's white—of Caucasian racial
background from the look of her" and the point may
become more clear; the racial or cultural background
of Professor Andover is not relevant here.]

> *revised* I've heard that Professor Andover's course
> in Canadian literature is very interesting.
> She just joined the department this year,
> apparently she's an expert on Leonard
> Cohen and the connections between lit-
> erature and music.

It's one thing to acknowledge this principle; it's quite another
to put it into practice, since in many cases doing so goes
against the habits of a lifetime. For most North Americans,
the only thing that might be thought of as objectionable in
the following passage from David Sedaris's highly amusing
autobiographical essay "Guy Walks into a Bar Car" is the
loud man's off-color joke:

> When a couple of seats opened up, Johnny and
> I took them. Across the narrow carriage, a black
> man with a bushy mustache pounded on the For-
> mica tabletop. "So a nun goes into town," he said,
> "and sees a sign reading, 'Quickies—Twenty-five
> Dollars.' Not sure what it means, she walks back to

the convent and pulls aside the mother superior. 'Excuse me,' she asks, 'but what's a quickie?

"And the old lady goes, 'Twenty-five dollars. Just like in town.'"

As the car filled with laughter, Johnny lit a fresh cigarette. "Some comedian," he said.

Sedaris's account of the train journey unfolds over several pages. The man with the mustache continues to tell crude jokes—and Sedaris continues to identify him not as as *the man with the bushy mustache* or *the loud man*—but as *the black man*—even as other (presumably white) people are identified in other ways:

"All right," called the black man on the other side of the carriage. "I've got another one." … A red-nosed woman in a decorative sweatshirt started to talk, but the black fellow told her that he wasn't done yet … As the black man settled down,…

"Here's a clean one," the black man said.…

But why should it matter, you may ask. Maybe his blackness is what the writer has noticed first about the man. Isn't that harmless enough? The short answer is no. If writers identify people first and foremost by their race and not by other, more individualized characteristics, they subtly color perceptions—both their readers' and their own. And that is of course particularly harmful when the characterization is a negative one. Sedaris is a wonderful writer, but in this instance he would have been a better writer had he referred repeatedly to *the mustachioed man* (or *the loudmouth*) and not to *the black man*. If North American history included the mass enslavement of mustachioed men or loudmouthed men, the point might be argued rather differently. But it doesn't.

Our internalized prejudices can also cause us, when we describe individuals, to emphasize the characteristics that reinforce those prejudices while deemphasizing characteristics that don't match our expectations. Consider the following descriptions of political candidates of different genders who have essentially the same backgrounds:

- Carla Jenkins, a lawyer and a school board trustee, is also the mother of three lovely daughters.
- George Kaplan, a lawyer and a school board trustee, has a long record of public service in the region.
- George Kaplan, a lawyer and a school board trustee, is also the father of three lovely daughters.
- Carla Jenkins, a lawyer and a school board trustee, has a long record of public service in the region.

The impression left in many minds by such phrasings is that the person described as having a long record of public service is well suited to public office, while the person whose parenting is emphasized may be better suited to staying at home. Some may feel that parenthood is relevant in such cases; if you do, be sure to mention it for everyone, not just for women. The guideline here is that, when describing a person, you should mention only the qualities you feel are relevant. And be sure to describe everyone you discuss in the same context with the same lens: if you feel it necessary to refer to relationship status or physical appearance, do so for everyone; if you mention degree qualifications or career achievements, do so for everyone.

Nor is it generally appropriate to stereotype members of particular groups even in ways that one considers positive; by doing so one may fail to give credit for individual achievement, while leaving the harmful impression that the given group possesses innate qualities that are universal among members of the group.

needs checking   Of course she gets straight As in all her subjects; she's from Hong Kong.

revised   It's no wonder she gets straight As in all her subjects; her parents have given her a great deal of encouragement, and she works very hard.

It's clear, then, that we should not overemphasize a person's race, gender, or membership in any other group in ways that reinforce stereotypes about that group. But what about situations where a person's membership in a given group contradicts common stereotypes? Certainly, you would not want to call attention to the fact that a certain police officer is black or a certain pastor is bisexual every time you mentioned that person. But it is also important to keep in mind that "police officer" and "pastor" are two of many descriptors that, for most people, carry with them a harmful set of default assumptions—in these cases, that, unless we are told otherwise, any given police officer or minister is a white, heterosexual man. Even those of us who try to avoid being prejudiced tend to have internalized assumptions like these. If we try to ignore them by pretending that race, gender, and other differences do not exist, we risk perpetuating the "default" status of whiteness, maleness, and so on.

Some people may pride themselves on being "colorblind" when it comes to race, for example, or on thinking that gay and heterosexual people are "just the same." But just as it is a worthy goal not to overemphasize differences, it is important not to overlook them entirely, as though the vast differences between the life experiences of human beings were insignificant or embarrassing. Acknowledging difference is important, in large part, because many differences come with relative degrees of privilege and prejudice attached, and ignoring difference is often tantamount to ignoring discrimination. But recognizing difference is also important simply because human beings are not all the same, and all experiences ought to be acknowledged—not just the experiences of the "default" race, gender, sexual orientation, religion, class, size, and so on. Audre Lorde, an important Black lesbian feminist theorist of the twentieth century, suggested that the acknowledgment and even celebration of difference was central to combatting prejudice:

> [W]e have *all* been programmed to respond to the human differences between us with fear and loathing and to handle that difference in one of three ways: ignore it, and if that is not possible copy it if we think it is dominant, or destroy it if we think it is subordinate. But we have no patterns for relating across our human differences as equals....
>
> Certainly there are very real differences between us of race, age, and sex. But it is not those

differences between us that are separating us. It is rather our refusal to recognize those differences.[1] ...

Some of us might find it more comfortable to avoid talking and writing about difference entirely, but that is not something we can afford to do. *How* exactly we can best talk about specific differences is one of the major questions addressed in the rest of this book.

introduction

---

1   "Age, Race, Class, and Sex: Women Redefining Difference," *Sister Outsider*, 1984.

CLASS

Here's another example of a widely used expression that is strongly colored with bias: the expression *white trash*. It's an expression that's problematic from more than one angle. The suggestion that any group of people can be referred to as "trash" is in itself problematic, of course. But there's more to it than that. The full implications of the expression are brought forward in the following passage:

> The [Jerry Lee] Lewis and [Jimmy] Swaggart clans were, in the harsh modern parlance, white trash. They lived in the black part of town, and had close relations with blacks. Mr. Swaggart's preaching and Mr. Lewis's music were strongly influenced by black culture. "Jimmy Swaggart was as black as a white man can be," said black elders in Ferriday.[1]

This passage brings out very clearly the implication of the expression; the "trashiness" that is the exception for white people is implicitly regarded as the norm for Black people. Yet, remarkably, mainstream white America continues to use the expression as if it were ethically unproblematic. The September 2016 cover of *The Atlantic* magazine, for example, carried the heading *White Trash* on its cover—without quotation marks or any other acknowledgment that the phrase carries deep levels of bias within it. The piece mentioned on the magazine cover was a review article focused in large part on historian Nancy Isenberg's book *White Trash: The 400-Year Untold History of Class in America*—which again carries no quotation marks around the expression "White

---

1 "The Godcousin," *The Economist*, 15 April 2000.

Trash" to indicate that it is being referenced as a historical artifact rather than an unexceptionable phrase that may be used without any qualms today.

The expression *that's so ghetto* brings together class and race in a similar way. Used to describe something that is makeshift or shoddily put together, the expression carries the implication that such is the norm for African Americans living in poor neighborhoods. It's an expression that's derogatory both towards poor people and towards Black people, and it should be avoided.

Just as objectionable are the numerous terms that have been used as slurs against low-income white people— *cracker*, *hillbilly*, and so on. But what of the term *redneck*? Originally an uncomplimentary term used to denote white male farmers with low incomes and little education (especially those living in the Southern United States, and in Canada's prairie provinces), *redneck* has shifted its meaning somewhat over the years. It's now used more frequently than ever, even as farmers in North America have come to constitute less than 1% of the population (and have become far better off financially than was once the case). Nowadays, of course, *redneck* is not only used in reference to those who might actually get their necks red working outdoors in the hot sun every day; it's often used with reference to whites who hold right-wing views and who do not hold any university or college degree—regardless of what job they may work at or where they may live. Though for many people *redneck* retains its derogatory connotations, many others embrace it proudly, describing themselves as *rednecks* and taking the term to imply less a set of specific political views than a set of social values—placing a high value on working hard and playing hard, and on loyalty to partner, family,

class

and community—and, just as importantly, to imply a rejection of the pretentious ways of the rich and sophisticated. (This set of meanings finds full expression in such country music standards as Gretchen Wilson's "Redneck Woman" and Blake Shelton's "Boys Round Here.") Those who still look to use the term *redneck* as a derogatory slur meaning "low-income white males whose views I disagree with" are advised to exercise caution!

The inappropriateness of using expressions such as *white trash*, *that's so ghetto* and *redneck* as slurs on other people's behavior is often acknowledged. Less widely understood is the degree to which various expressions that are often used to describe wealthy people carry class baggage. Think, for example, of expressions such as these:

- She comes from a good family.
- He's making a good income now.
- By some definitions the couple may not be rich, but they are certainly well-off.

A centuries-old tradition among the rich and the middle class in North American and European culture holds that it is vulgar to refer to oneself or to friends and acquaintances as rich. For generations it has been accepted among the wealthy (and among many who aspire to wealth) that in most situations one should use euphemisms when referring to wealth and income. Many euphemisms do no harm, of course. But when one uses phrases such as *good family* to mean *rich family*, one is subtly coloring the financial with the moral. By implication, such phrasings further disadvantage those already disadvantaged by poverty, lending it a taint of a moral as well as a financial shortfall. Of course a phrase such as *good family* can also be used in contexts

class

where wealth is not implied; the phrase can be and is often applied to families that are not rich. But those who believe that it's preferable to make one's meaning clear (and who believe that poverty is not evidence of any moral failing) are well advised to exercise care with such terms, and consider using more precise wording:

- She comes from a family that has long been regarded as wealthy and respectable.
  [if one means to convey that the family is wealthy]
- She comes from a family that is very well regarded in the community.
  [if one is using the phrase without any connotation of wealth]
- He's making a large amount of money now.
- By some definitions the couple may not be rich, but they own a summer place as well as a large house in town, and most years they manage a vacation in Europe.

worth checking The novel focuses on a woman who comes from a good family in New York; when the family falls on hard times, she faces difficult choices.

revised The novel focuses on a woman who has moved in wealthy circles in New York; when her family falls on hard times, she faces difficult choices.

class

Even when you are using accepted terminology to discuss class, it is good to keep in mind the effects your word choice might have. *Lower class*, for example, is a widely used term that suggests a negative value judgment; descriptors such as *working class* (where appropriate) and *low-income* are usually preferable.

Questions and Suggestions for Discussion

1. Explore the etymology (and discuss the appropriateness of) the expression *making good money*. As well, using the Ngram viewer,[1] check the historical pattern as to how frequently the term has been used.

2. Using the Ngram viewer, compare (and comment on) the frequency with which the expression *living from paycheck to paycheck* has been used since 1975.

3. Using the Ngram viewer, compare (and comment on) the frequency with which *upper class*, *lower class*, *working class*, and *middle class* have been used since 1800.

4. Using the Ngram viewer, compare (and comment on) the frequency with which *classy* and *low class* have been used.

5. Using the *Oxford English Dictionary*, explore the change in meaning of the adjective *condescending* that occurred in the nineteenth and twentieth centuries.

class

---

1   For a quick introduction to the Ngram viewer, see the section entitled "How to Use This Book" at the beginning of the volume.

DISABILITY

There has long been uncertainty about how best to speak of disabilities in general, as well as about how best to speak of individual people who have particular disabilities. Terms such as *cripple* and *mentally retarded* have since the late twentieth century come to be universally regarded as derogatory, but there is a great deal of ongoing discussion as to the specific terms that have been put forward as replacements. It is rightly believed that we should use terms that do not suggest a person's disability to be greater than is in fact the case; we should use terminology that avoids reducing individuals or groups of people to their disabilities. If someone is described as *a disabled person*, it is easy to see how the assumption may take root that the person is *entirely* disabled—unable to function in human society or contribute usefully in the world. But in the other direction, terms such as *differently abled*, *physically challenged*, and *mentally challenged* strike many as euphemisms devoid of any content suggesting the nature or extent of what are often very serious issues faced by people with disabilities. No two people have precisely the same abilities, and everyone faces challenges in life, both mental and physical; what's so special about having different abilities, or facing challenges? One common approach is to use phrasing that begins with *person* or *people*; consider the phrase *people with disabilities*, and how it differs from *the disabled*. So too with individuals: whereas saying "she is disabled" might be taken to suggest the person you are speaking of is incapable of making a

disability

significant contribution, saying "she has a disability" suggests nothing of the sort.[1]

As with gender and race or cultural background, there is no need to mention a disability unless it is relevant to the topic of discussion.

needs checking   Professor Caswell joined the History Department in 2006. A distinguished scholar, he is the author of several books on early American society. He's confined to a wheelchair, though.
[If you are outlining Professor Caswell's credentials and accomplishments, his physical disability is not something you need to mention.]

revised   Professor Caswell joined the History Department in 2006. A distinguished scholar, he is the author of several books on early American society.

Notice also how the reference to the wheelchair is worded in the above example. Phrases such as "confined to a wheelchair" can subtly color people's judgments as to whether or not someone will be an asset to a community, or a burden on it.

needs checking   People on campus often notice that Professor Caswell is confined to a wheelchair.

revised   People on campus often notice that Professor Caswell gets around in a wheelchair.

---

1   There are some exceptions to this approach; many members of the Deaf community, for example, embrace this identity and prefer to be described simply as Deaf. See the discussion of identity-first language elsewhere in this section.

retard/retarded

One important issue regarding people with cognitive or other intellectual disabilities is the careless use of the words *retarded* and *retard*. Virtually everyone understands that these are pejorative terms that should not be used with reference to people with disabilities. But many continue to use the term *retarded* as a synonym for *stupid*. When such terms are not directed at other people they may seem harmless, but they have the effect of reinforcing unfortunate associations.

needs checking	That was totally retarded of me; I knew the answer and I just couldn't think of it.
revised	That was totally stupid of me; I knew the answer and I just couldn't think of it.
needs checking	My computer is so retarded; now it won't even let me attach a document to this email.
revised	My computer is completely malfunctioning; now it won't even let me exit the program.
or	[if the circumstances seem to demand personifying the computer] My computer is so stupid; now it won't even let me exit the program.

disability

CASES TO CONSIDER

Identity-First Language:
Exceptions to the Person-First Rule

Though a good general rule for discussing disability is to use person-first language—to say, for example, *people with epilepsy* rather than *epileptic people*—there are some exceptions to this rule. These exceptions tend to occur when groups of people with traits commonly considered disabilities consider those traits to be a core part of their identity—and, in some cases, traits they would not describe as disabilities at all.

One example of this occurs in the Deaf community, which is a linguistic minority culture (one that, in the United States and English-speaking Canada, uses American Sign Language, which has its own grammar independent of English). *Deaf* with a capital *D* indicates membership in this culture and is an important identity marker for most participants in the culture. It would be rude to de-emphasize this identity marker by using people-first language—to say *people who are Deaf*. The appropriate thing, as with any group with an identity the group's members want to foreground, is to use identity-first language: to say *Deaf people*.

The meaning of *Deaf* with a capital *D* is distinct from the meaning of *deaf* with a lowercase *d*, which refers specifically to hearing ability; someone who is *deaf* can hear very little or nothing at all, while *hard of hearing* describes someone who can hear only with difficulty, but has more hearing ability than a deaf person. (*Hard of hearing* is also, however, used in practice by some people who are technically deaf but want to make it clear that they are not part of the Deaf community.) Someone who almost completely lost her hearing late in life and does not participate in the Deaf community might describe herself as deaf or hard of hearing but not Deaf, while someone who can hear a little bit more but signs and is part of the Deaf community might describe himself as Deaf and as hard of hearing. It is appropriate to use identity-first language—*hard of hearing people*, *deaf people*, etc.—in all of these cases.

A related issue is the common phrase *hearing impaired*, which it is best not to use.[1] The word *impaired* suggests a lack or limitation and frames deafness negatively in terms of disability, when many Deaf people do not see it that way and are just as able to communicate using Sign as the users of any other language. *Hearing impaired* describes a physical lack as perceived by the hearing community; *Deaf* describes membership in a culture in which not hearing is not a problem.

A much more controversial question regards autism: should we use the phrase *people with autism* or the phrase *autistic people*? Some advocates—including many neurotypical parents of children with autism and many people with autism who feel they have an illness—argue that autism is an illness, not an integral part of the personality of someone with autism. According to this argument, *people with autism* is best because it emphasizes the humanity of those who have the illness rather than emphasizing the illness itself. The dominant position among members of the autistic self-

---

1   Some people use *hearing impaired* to describe themselves—these are usu-
    ally people who have lost hearing as they aged and feel their hearing loss is
    accurately described as an impairment. Most advocates view this as a reason-
    able exception, but *hard of hearing* is still usually the best way to describe
    people with later-life hearing loss if you don't know an individual's preference
    or if you are describing a group.

advocacy movement, on the other hand, is that both *autistic people* and *autistics* should be used. This position reflects the belief that autism is an integral part of an autistic person's self, and that "curing" someone of it would be tantamount to erasing that individual's personality. The phrase *people with autism*, according to this argument, falsely implies that autism is a disease that can be separated from the autistic individual, and that it therefore ought to be cured. Lydia Brown, in her article "Identity-First Language" on the Autistic Self Advocacy Network website, argues persuasively for this view:

> When we say "person with autism," we say that it is unfortunate and an accident that a person is Autistic. We affirm that the person has value and worth, and that autism is entirely separate from what gives him or her value and worth. In fact, we are saying that autism is detrimental to value and worth as a person, which is why we separate the condition with the word "with" or "has." Ultimately, what we are saying when we say "person with autism" is that the person would be better off if not Autistic, and that it would have been better if he or she had been born typical....
>
> Yet, when we say "Autistic person," we recognize, affirm, and validate an individual's identity as an Autistic person.... We affirm the individual's potential to grow and mature, to overcome challenges and disability, and to live a meaningful life *as an Autistic*. Ultimately, we are accepting that the individual is different from non-Autistic people— and that that's not a tragedy.

Opposing Views on Language and Mental Illness

Laura's View:

Of all the stigmatizing words still commonly used in conversation by people of all political stripes, those relating to mental illness are among the most common. (They were until recently used by all three of this book's authors.) Expressions such as *That guy was a psycho* or *I'm totally OCD about my bookshelf* are so commonplace as to be hardly noticeable—but what is it about words such as *crazy, nuts,* and so on that make them seem acceptable, even in some circles where words such as *retarded* are clearly not? One explanation—one I have increasingly come to believe is the right one—is that mental illnesses are still so heavily stigmatized in North American culture that people don't think twice about language that dehumanizes people who have these illnesses. *Crazy* and many related words may not be in general official use anymore (though *insane* still is). They are, however, certainly still in use as an insult for people who have mental illnesses—or who the speaker wants to dismiss as having a mental illness (*That woman who yelled at me for taking the last watermelon was crazy; My landlord is totally nuts*). I have also heard people with mental illnesses identify themselves as *crazy*—some reclaiming the word in a spirit of rebellion, others using it as a slur in moments of self-loathing.

The unacceptability of *crazy, insane,* and so on as slurs may seem relatively obvious, but what of situations where such words are used when we aren't talking about people? Here, too, I have come around to the view that these words are harmful because they perpetuate the stigma and stereo-

disability

types attached to mental illness. Imagine that you're talking to someone with a mental illness. (You often are, whether you know it or not—mental illness is extremely common in the United States and Canada.[1]) Given how difficult it already is to ask for help, or to tell others about having a mental illness, do people with mental illnesses really need to be reminded that society views them as wholly divorced from reality (*That tax proposal was nuts*), incapable of ethical behavior (*I'm a dog person because cats are psycho*), outside the everyday (*That party was insane*), extreme (*I'm crazy busy*), and at the mercy of their emotions (*I'm crazy about you*)?

Part of the reason that, as a lover of language, I used to use *crazy* and related words so frequently is that few words have the same evocative impact, or the same range of meanings. There is, as far as I can tell, no single word that can be used to replace *crazy* in every one of its uses—so some thought is required of English speakers who want to take up the challenge of eliminating these words from their everyday use. If you want to say *That tax proposal was nuts*, do you really mean that it was *bizarre*, or *full of lies*, or *completely nonsensical*? If *That party was insane*, could it also have been *wild*, or *outrageous*, or *extreme*? If you're feeling *crazy busy*, that might be more fun to say than *really busy*, but it strikes me as more important not to reduce others—or yourself, if you have a mental illness now or in the future—to a series of negative stereotypes.

---

1   According to the Canadian Mental Health Association's "Report on Mental Illnesses in Canada" (2002), 20 percent of Canadians will experience a mental illness in their lifetime. In the United States, numbers are even higher; according to the Congressional Research Service report "Prevalence of Mental Illness in the United States: Data Sources and Estimates" (Erin Bagalman and Angela Napili, 2015), between 25 and 32 percent of Americans experience a mental illness *in any given year*.

Don's View:

Laura reports that she has "heard people with mental ill-nesses identify themselves as *crazy*—some reclaiming the word in a spirit of rebellion, others using it as a slur in moments of self-loathing." But this does not exhaust the possibilities. Specific cases can certainly help to sharpen perceptions over this sort of issue. I think of my grand-mother, who was hospitalized with what were then called paranoid delusions; of my mother, who died of Alzhei-mer's some years ago; and of an extraordinarily bright and extraordinarily kind philosopher who was for years among my closest friends and who died in his mid-sixties, also of a form of Alzheimer's. I don't claim to be able to remember conversations with complete accuracy, but it certainly seems to me that Dennis would often quietly say things like "I went a bit crazy there" with reference, for example, to periods in which he had been screaming and banging his head against a wall. In the wake of such incidents I would hug him and try to reassure him that things were all right again now—and I may well have agreed with him that he had *gone a bit crazy* when he had been banging his head against the wall and screaming over and over that he didn't deserve to live. Was either one of us perpetuating the stigma and stereotypes attached to mental illness when we used that phrase? I honestly don't think we were—though I readily acknowledge that, used in different contexts and in a different tone, *crazy* can indeed be an unacceptable slur.

To say *I went a bit crazy* is to use an expression that blurs the lines between mental states that are manifestations of illness and mental states that are entirely within the realm of healthy behavior. People often use the expression *I went*

disability

a bit crazy, for example, to describe their enthusiastic cheering when their favorite team has won a big game. More broadly, the word and its derivatives have an extraordinarily wide range of meanings (*the tulip craze, the hula-hoop craze, those crazy kids, I'm crazy in love for the first time*)—many of them about as far as can be imagined from the reality of serious mental illness. For someone in Dennis's position to use such a term, then, can be simultaneously to acknowledge and to downplay the severity of the problem. In such a context it is a phrase that allows scope for nuance—and certainly in Dennis's case, for a gentle half-ironic smile. And for language to provide that flexibility, that openness to nuance, seems to me to be a good thing—a healthy thing.

The word *crazy* is certainly not alone in this respect; in Shakespeare's day, of course, someone with mental illness would be referred to as *mad* or as a *fool* rather than as a *crazy person.* As anyone who has read or seen *King Lear* must know, those words too—*mad, fool, foolish*—have a rich history that allows an extraordinary amount of room for nuance. They remain words that can be used as slurs,[1] but they have so many other meanings and contribute in so many ways to the richness of the language that it would be unimaginable to consider them as unacceptable terms.

Certain other words relating to mental illness or cognitive disability—among them *imbecile, lunatic,* and *retarded*—have come with good reason to occupy the other end of the spectrum, much as they may have been launched with the best of intentions. The use of *retarded person* with

---

1   The meanings of the words have shifted somewhat over the centuries, of course. Whereas *mad* (and *madman*) are still sometimes used as insults relating to mental illness, fool and foolish no longer are; if someone today calls another person *a stupid fool* no one would imagine that the insult is meant to imply mental illness.

disability

reference to disability, for example, began as part of a well-intentioned effort to find gentler, kinder, alternatives to terms such as *idiot*. But *retarded* came fairly quickly to be used almost purely in a pejorative sense. Moreover, it possesses nothing like the same rich history as do *mad*, *foolish*, and *crazy*; *retarded* lacks the sort of diversity of meaning through which those words have so enriched the language. For the present at least, we have nothing to lose and much to gain by categorizing such words as unacceptable slurs. To my mind, *crazy* is much closer to *mad* and *foolish* in these respects than it is to *retarded*.

Language changes in often unpredictable ways, of course; perhaps in another hundred years *retarded* will have been reclaimed by people categorized as having a mental disability, and *crazy* will have lost a good deal of its richness and nuance—in which case there will be a much stronger case than there is now for consigning *crazy* to the dustbin.

Questions and Suggestions for Discussion

1. Using the *Oxford English Dictionary*, explore the etymology of the expression *mentally retarded*. As well, using the Ngram viewer,[1] check (and comment on) the historical pattern as to how frequently the term has been used.

2. Using the Ngram viewer, compare (and comment on) the frequency with which the expression *differently abled* was used from 1975 through 2008. How do you explain the decline in the term's use since 1995?

---

1   For a quick introduction to the Ngram viewer, see the section entitled "How to Use This Book" at the beginning of the volume.

3. Using the Ngram viewer, compare (and comment on) the frequency with which the term *crippled children* has been used from 1880 onwards. In a separate Ngram view, check the historical use of the term *crippled civilians*. You may also wish to explore the etymological history of the *Society for Crippled Civilians* charity in Toronto. Why would civilians have been specified in the agency's name? Are you surprised by the date of the change to *Goodwill Industries*?

GENDER

The healthy revolution in attitudes towards gender roles in recent generations has created some awkwardness in English usage—though not nearly so much as some have claimed. *Chair* is a simple non-sexist replacement for *chairman*, as is *business people* for *businessmen*. No one is forced into using *garbageperson* or *policeperson*; *police officer* and *garbage collector* are entirely unobjectionable, even to the linguistic purist. Nor can the purist complain if *fisher* replaces *fisherman*; far from being a new or artificial coinage, *fisher* was linguistic currency when the King James version of the Bible was written in the early seventeenth century. Here again, there is no need for the *-person* suffix. (For more on *fisher*, see the case study below.)

The use of *mankind* to mean *humanity*, and of *man* to mean *human being*, have for some years been rightly frowned upon. Ironically enough, *man* originally had *human being* as its only meaning; in Old English a *werman* was a male adult human being, a *wifman* a female. It was not until after the Norman Conquest in 1066 that the word *man* began to do double duty—to be used both to mean *human being* and to mean *male human being*. No doubt inevitably, that lopsided pattern of usage fostered a bias towards the masculine in the word *man*. That male bias became powerfully reinforced over the centuries—until finally, in the twentieth century, the use of *man* to mean *human being* or *humankind* came to be broadly recognized as biased towards the male—sexist, in other words. Broadly recognized, but not universally: a remarkable number of adults still cling to these sexist usages. A few openly prefer to use a word that is biased towards male people, while others manage to persuade themselves that it remains possible to use *man* in a gender-neutral fashion.

Among them are the editors of at least one of the world's leading magazines. More than a decade and a half into the twenty-first century, the majority of reputable English-language newspapers and magazines use words such as *people* or *humanity* when they are referring to everyone. *The Economist* and a few others, though, still stick to the old ways. Back in their 14 September 1996 issue, the magazine's editors posed the question "What Is Man?" in their lead article. "To what extent are men's actions determined by their genes?" the article asked, and clearly did not intend the answer to apply to only one-half the human race. They have continued the same practice through to the present; a 22 January 2015 article bore the headline, "The whole family of man."

Well, why can't *man* be gender neutral? To start with, because of the historical baggage such usage carries with it. Here, for example, is what the best-selling novelist Grant Allen had to say on the topic in a magazine called *Forum* in 1889:

> In man, I would confidently assert, as biological fact, the males are the race; the females are merely the sex told off to recruit and reproduce it. All that is distinctly human is man—the field, the ship, the mine, the workshop; all that is truly woman is merely reproductive—the home, the nursery, the schoolroom.

But the baggage is not merely historical; much of the problem remains embedded in the language today. A useful litmus test is how sex and gender differences are approached. Look, for example, at this sentence from that 14 September 1996 issue of *The Economist*:

- One of the most basic distinctions in human experience—that between men and women—is getting blurrier and blurrier.

Now let's try the same sentence using *man's* instead of *human*:

- One of the most basic distinctions in man's experience—that between men and women—is getting blurrier and blurrier.

In this sort of context we are all forced to sense that something is amiss. We have to realize when we see such examples that *man* and *he* and even *mankind* inevitably carry with them some whiff of maleness; they can never fully and fairly represent all of humanity. (If they didn't carry with them some scent of maleness it wouldn't be possible to make a joke about the difficulty of turning men into human beings.) Most contexts are of course more subtle than this, and it is thus often easy for humans—but especially for men—not to notice that the male terms always carry with them connotations that are not gender-neutral. *Humanity, humans, people*—these words are not in any way awkward or jargon-ridden; let's use them.

inappropriate	Mankind cannot bear very much reality.
gender neutral	Humankind cannot bear very much reality.
	–T.S. Eliot, *Murder in the Cathedral*, (and also *Four Quartets*)

On the same grounds, it of course makes sense to say *police officers* instead of *policemen*, and *salespeople* (or *sales clerks* or *sales representatives*) instead of *salesmen*. But what of less obvious words that have *man* or *men* embedded within them? What of *man*ual, or *man*ipulate, or *Man*itoba? If we are to find substitutes for *policeman* and *salesman*, should we not also find replacements for these words? Should we not, as more than a few wags have sarcastically suggested, start saying *personipulate* and *Personitoba*? "But wait!" the satirist is likely to continue. "Look at the -*son* in *person*. We mustn't have male bias of that sort! Surely we had better say *peroffspringulate* and *Peroffspringitoba*. Shouldn't we?"

The short answer to that, of course, is no. And not only because of the awkwardness of such words. Constructions of this sort are "solutions" to a problem that never existed. In any meaningful sense, there is no maleness embedded in the noun *Manitoba*, for *Manitoba* does not mean "place of man" or anything of that sort. It derives from words in a First Nations language (probably the Cree words *manitowapau*, meaning *strait of the Spirit*). The word *manual* stems from the Latin *manus*, meaning hand, rather than from any word having to do with gender—and there should thus be no suggestion of manual work being for males only. And the word *person*? It stems not from anything having to do with a male child but rather from the Latin *persona*, meaning *human being*. In any meaningful sense, there is not in fact a son in *person*.

The same sort of etymological confusion lies at the heart of any suggestion that we should regard it as problematic that there is a -*man* in *human*, and a -*man* in *woman*, and a -*male* in *female*. The word *human* derives from the Latin words *humanus* and *humana*, meaning "of or relating to the human." The word *female* comes to us not from anything to do with masculinity but from the Latin *femella*, meaning *girl*. The word *male*, on the other hand, comes from the Old French *masle*, which in turn comes from the Latin *masculus*—both meaning masculine. (Along the way we may as well point out that the word for *bad* in French is *mal*, but that there is no *mal* in *male*, any more than there is any *ale* in *male*—or in *female*, for that matter.)

pronouns and gender neutrality

To replace *man* with *humanity* is not inherently awkward to even a slight degree. But the pronouns are more difficult. Clearly the consistent use of *he* to represent both sexes is unacceptable. Yet *he/she*, *s/he*, and *he or she* are undeniably awkward. *S/he* is quite functional on the printed page, but defies translation into oral English. Another solution is to avoid the singular pronoun as much as possible either by repeating nouns (*An architect should be aware of the architect's clients' budgets as well as the architect's grand schemes*) or by switching to the plural (*Architects should be aware of their clients' budgets as well as of their own grand schemes*). Of these two the second is obviously preferable. In longer works some prefer a third strategy that eliminates awkwardness entirely: to alternate between the masculine pronoun *he* and the feminine pronoun *she* when referring to a single, generic member of a group. Using *she* to refer to, say, an architect, or a professor, or a sports star, or a prime minister can have the salutary effect of reminding readers or listeners that there is nothing inherently male in these occupations. In a short piece of writing, however, it can be distracting

gender

to the reader if there are several bounces back and forth between female and male in the same paragraph. And a cautionary note should accompany this strategy even when it may conveniently be employed: be very careful not to assign *he* to all the professors, executives, or doctors; and *she* to all the students, secretaries, or nurses.

One of the most troublesome questions for those who are concerned about gender equality and about good English arises over situations involving singular pronouns such as *everyone, anyone, anybody, somebody, someone, no one, each, either,* and *neither.* Consider the following sentence:

- Everybody said that they thought this was the best film they had seen all year.

If we don't accept the use of the singular "they," that sentence is grammatically wrong; according to rules that many grammarians regard as unbendable, *everybody* is singular, and *they* must therefore be changed:

- Everybody said that he or she thought this was the best film he or she had seen all year.
- All the moviegoers said that they thought this was the best film each of them had seen all year.

But there are a growing number of writers who have become frustrated with the contortions involved in such approaches to avoiding sexism. Why should we have to rephrase sentences to use the plural "they," such writers ask, or alternate between "he" and "she" when neither fully reflects our meaning? Such writers suggest that the problem is really with the current grammar of the English language, which is missing a necessary word: a gender-neutral singular pronoun that is appropriate to use for human beings. *It* is gender-neutral but offensive to most people; some writers have coined new pronouns such as *ze*, but many English speakers are uncomfortable with such unfamiliar words and their usage has not become widespread. To find a pronoun that serves the purpose and feels natural to most English speakers, writers have looked to the history of the language, where for many centuries there was in fact a gender-neutral pronoun that had long been used in singular form: *they*. First recorded in the late fourteenth century, the singular *they* is used by such authors as Chaucer, Shakespeare, Jane Austen, and Bernard Shaw:

> "But remember that the pain of parting from friends will be felt by every body at times, whatever be **their** education or state."
> –Jane Austen, *Sense and Sensibility*

> There's not a man I meet but doth salute me
> As if I were **their** well-acquainted friend....
> –William Shakespeare, *A Comedy of Errors*

This usage came to be considered incorrect as part of the codification of English grammar that took root in the eighteenth century. In 1745 the grammarian Ann Fisher claimed that *he* ought to be used instead of *they* in gender-neutral situations because, she argued in her *New Grammar and Spelling Book*, "[t]he Masculine Person ... comprehends both Male and Female." By the nineteenth century, both aspects of this rule—the unacceptability of the singular *they* and the acceptability of *he* for gender-neutral use—were widely agreed upon for formal writing on the grounds of number agreement: singular words require singular pronouns. The singular *they* persisted, however, in informal speech, where it remains very common.

And as the twenty-first century advances, the singular *they* is again becoming more common in formal writing. In 2015 the *Washington Post* changed its official policy to accept the singular *they*, which the *Post*'s copy editor called "the only sensible solution to English's lack of a gender-neutral third-person singular personal pronoun."[1] The singular *they* has been adopted by the Australian government for use in legal documents, and is recommended in the Canadian Department of Justice's guide to drafting legislation.[2] In January 2016, the linguists of the American Dialect Society recognized this linguistic shift by declaring the singular *they* 2015's Word of the Year. As John McIntyre, former president of the American Copy Editors Society, has argued, we do indeed need a gender-neutral third-person singular personal pronoun, "but we already have one, and it's *they*."[3]

It does appear that the tide is turning, and the singular "they" may well become an acceptable part of formal English everywhere, but it is worth noting that this has not yet occurred. Even the *Washington Post* still recommends that writers "recast sentences as plural" where possible and only use *they* when "such a rewrite is impossible or hopelessly awkward."[4] Many style guides—including the official guides for Chicago Style and APA Style—still reject the singular "they" as ungrammatical. Some experts, such as the linguist

---

1   See Bill Walsh, "The Post Drops the 'Mike'—and the Hyphen in 'E-Mail,'" *The Washington Post*, 4 December 2015.
2   See "Legistics: Singular They" on the Canadian Department of Justice website.
3   See Lauren Klinger and Kristen Hare, "Question from ACES2015: Is It Time to Accept 'They' as a Singular Pronoun?," *Poynter*, 2 April 2015.
4   See Benjamin Mullin, "*The Washington Post* Will Allow Singular 'They,'" *Poynter*, 1 December 2015.

but here again, it is important not to refer unnecessarily to biology, and never to imply through your language that anyone is not "really" their identified gender.

needs checking   Jan Morris, born a man, became famous as James Morris, the author of *Pax Britannica*; since 1972 she has publicly identified as a woman, and become even more famous as a travel writer.

[The *Pax Britannica* trilogy is still variously listed as having been written by Jan Morris or by James Morris; to identify Jan Morris as the author is now preferred practice.]

revised   Jan Morris became famous as James Morris, the author of *Pax Britannica*; since 1972 she has publicly identified as a woman, and become even more famous as a travel writer.

[The *Pax Britannica* trilogy is still variously listed as having been written by Jan Morris or by James Morris; to identify Jan Morris as the author is now preferred practice.]

Where possible, when addressing or referring to specific individuals, it is best to follow their own preferences regarding terminology and pronouns; while one transgender person might want to be called a *trans woman*, a *transsexual woman*, or simply a *woman* and prefer *she/her* pronouns, another person might identify as *genderqueer*[1] and prefer

1   The term *genderqueer* includes people who identify as without gender, as both male and female, as having a fluid gender that changes over time, as having more than two genders, or as anything else other than strictly "male" (cont'd)

gender-neutral pronouns such as *they/them* or *ze/hir*. It is always best to use an individual's preferred pronouns, but, as with gender in general, there is no need to mention someone's non-normative gender status unless it is relevant to the subject being discussed.

"they" as a pronoun for individuals

People with nonbinary genders use a variety of pronouns— from the conventional *he/him* or *she/her* to invented pronouns such as *ze/hir*, *ey/em*, and *ne/nem*. One of the most common choices is *they/them*. The use of *they* as a singular pronoun is controversial when it is not in reference to a specific person (e.g., *Everybody should do their taxes*; see the discussion above)—and, in some quarters at least,[1] it's even more controversial to use *they* as a singular pronoun in reference to a specific individual. But when a specific person has requested that the pronoun *they* be used to refer to them, our view is that doing your best to accommodate their request is the only respectful approach.

When using *they* to refer to a specific individual, conjugating the verbs can be slightly tricky. The standard approach is to use the singular verb when referring to them by name, and the plural when using the pronoun.

---

or "female." Though we have here included genderqueer identities under the umbrella of "transgender," it is worth noting that some activists argue that the transgender category should be reserved only for people who identify as "male" or "female" in opposition to the gender they were assigned at birth.

1   A good example is the reaction among conservative commentators to the University of Tennessee's declaration that the institution was open to the use of gender-neutral pronouns (while emphasizing that the use of these pronouns was not being mandated or required by the university). Fox News' Ted Starnes responded with a question ("I wonder if they've got a gender-neutral word for *idiot*?"), while evangelist Franklin Graham enlisted God in the fight against gender-neutral pronouns on college campuses ("God created male and female—you don't have to have a college degree to understand that").

needs checking   I know Jamie has their own homework, but does they have time to help me with mine?

needs checking   I know Jamie have their own homework, but do they have time to help me with mine?

revised   I know Jamie has their own homework, but do they have time to help me with mine?

The most commonly accepted reflexive pronoun in these cases is *themselves*, though some writers prefer to use *themself*:

Lindsay hurt themself playing hockey.

Lindsay hurt themselves playing hockey.

CASES TO CONSIDER

Opposing Views on Doing Our Best with Nonbinary Pronouns: How Much Is Enough?

Don's View:

It's with good reason that we refer above to "doing your best" to accommodate such requests, for linguists tell us that doing so is not easy. Linguists have found a significant distinction, apparently originating in the way language is processed by the human brain, between content words (such as nouns) and function words (such as pronouns). The former may be changed and added to without much difficulty, whereas the latter are highly resistant to change and innovation. As a result, we can train our minds to say *flight attendant* rather than *stewardess* fairly easily, but it is much more difficult for us to train ourselves to use new pronouns—and more difficult still to train ourselves to customize pronouns, using certain pronouns only for certain individuals. Daniel O'Donnell of the University of Lethbridge has summarized the issue in this way:

> … the laws of grammar make [pronouns] much harder to modify. They do change and they can be engineered (the Swedes recently created a new pronoun, "hen," to cover "not specifically male or female"). But they cannot be customized. This is because pronouns are, by their very nature, anti-individual. They are the parts of speech that are used to strip away the semantic qualities that make things, people and ideas unique.[1]

O'Donnell is surely right in pointing to a difficulty here. Where I part company with him (and with many others who are resistant when individuals request that they be referred to as *they* or as *ze* rather than as *he* or *she*) is in his assumption that customizing pronouns is a flat impossibility. The current practice of a significant number of people clearly suggests that's not the case—suggests that, much as customizing pronouns may present real cognitive challenges, it is not impossible for humans to use individual pronouns for individuals. If an individual asks you to refer to them as *they* or as *ze*, we recommend doing everything you can to honor that request. If it were to come to the point that everyone you knew were requesting you to use

---

1 Daniel O'Donnell, "Customized Pronouns: A Good Idea That Makes No Sense," *The Globe and Mail*, 15 October 2016.

a different individual pronoun in their particular case, it might indeed become a cognitive impossibility to honor all those requests. But, much as that sort of scenario is painted by various opponents of customizing pronouns, it hasn't happened, and it isn't likely to happen. Rather than focus on unlikely hypotheticals, let's simply do our best to honor individuals' pronoun requests.

Laura's View:

I take issue with the suggestion that to use a requested gender-neutral pronoun to refer to a person who is neither male nor female amounts to "customization" on an individual level. It's not; the adoption of an unfamiliar pronoun involves the creation of a new category—a pronoun used to refer to individuals of a particular category of gender—and then using it to refer to individuals of that category. Even if you happen to know only one person who tells you they identify with *ze/hir* or *they/them*, this doesn't make the use of correct pronouns any more a matter of individual "customization" than using "it" to refer to a backpack or "she" to refer to the Queen of England. This change in habit does require learning to use new pronouns, which may well be difficult. And to use these pronouns intuitively, one must accept the reality of nonbinary genders to the point that thinking of people as occupants of a particular nonbinary gender category becomes intuitive—which is certainly not a trivial learning process either!

There's no question that the difficulty of this learning process increases with the addition of each unfamiliar pronoun, and that it would be easier to refer to every nonbinary person as *they/them*, for example, than to learn to use *they/them* for one person and *ey/em* for someone else. But if the same set of pronouns simply doesn't match the gender experience of every nonbinary person, that means that English needs multiple sets of nonbinary pronouns—and of nonbinary gender categories—to acknowledge everyone's reality. Thinking of this as "customization" seems to me to be linked to all sorts of dangerous assumptions about gender—that, for example, people of nonbinary gender are just trying to be special (rather than to be referred to in a way that matches their genders, like binary people are), that experiences of nonbinary gender aren't real (so English doesn't need revised gender categories to incorporate them).

Pronouns' status as function words makes them an excellent illustration of the depth of the connection between our unconscious, socialized beliefs and the way that we speak and write. Changing our language to make it truly equal and inclusive with regard to subjects such as gender *is* difficult, because it requires that English speakers make fundamental changes in our linguistic categories, and in our categories of thought. It may be very hard, especially for those of us who are cisgender, to incorporate unfamiliar pronouns into our speech. But it really is *impossible* to truly acknowledge anyone's gender while using pronouns that misgender them. Meg Zulch, a genderqueer columnist, puts it this way:

> My pronouns are more than words. They are ideas. They reflect my gender, my being, my essence. And when you use the wrong one, when you say "she" and not "they," you're acknowledging that you don't see what I want you to see

when you look at me, the nonbinary androgynous person that I am. You erase me and say I'm too confusing to be able to begin to understand.[1]

Perhaps as our culture evolves and the use of nonbinary pronouns becomes more commonly accepted, one or a few sets of pronouns will become the standard, and it will become much more straightforward to acknowledge nonbinary genders. But until then there's really no excuse not to do the work of learning to use requested pronouns, to correct ourselves and apologize if we make mistakes, and to avoid treating any nonbinary person as though their request for appropriate pronouns is an imposition rather than an appeal for basic decency. As Zulch says,

> No cis woman with short hair wants to hear "sir," because odds are she identifies closely with her womanhood, and with her right to be called "her." But my frustration, and the frustration of other genderqueer people, feels like that too, yet it is always invalidated. We are told our pronouns are unnatural, confusing, or grammatically incorrect. And we are expected to be silently tolerant since our identity and simple requests are too damn confusing anyway for anyone to want to take the time to change one little word.

Freshmen and First-Year Students

Use of the word *freshman* to mean *first-year student at a university* is first recorded in the late sixteenth century; in the

---

1   "I Switched to Gender-Neutral Pronouns and This Is What I Learned," *Bustle*, 18 January 2016.

1590s Thomas Nashe writes of a young man as being "but yet a freshman in Cambridge" and a character in Thomas Dekker's play *The Roaring Girl* (c. 1607–10) is described as "a freshman and a sot"—in other words, a first-year student who is too fond of alcohol (a type quite unfamiliar to us today). At that point and for centuries afterwards, women were not typically allowed to attend university. That finally began to change in the second half of the nineteenth century, and nowadays women outnumber men at many post-secondary institutions. Not surprisingly, the term *freshman* has fallen into disuse in Britain; in that country (as in Australia,[1] Canada, and other English-speaking countries), first-year students are usually called exactly that—*first year students* (or, in informal usage, *a first-year*, plural *first-years*). In the United States, however, the term persists (as does the term *co-ed*, used as a noun to denote a female student—an odd term coined in the nineteenth century, when it was still a rare thing for institutions to be co-educational).

Is there any good reason to keep speaking of *freshmen* at universities and colleges? Should Americans (and those few Canadians who use the term) speak of *freshers* instead? Should the informal short form *frosh* be adopted in more formal contexts as an appropriate non-gendered substitute both for the singular *freshman* and the plural *freshmen*? Or should American universities finally accept *first-year students*?

Fisher or Fisherman?

On November 27, 2015, Kerry McCarthy, a prominent British Member of Parliament for the Labour Party, sent out

---

1   At a few Australian universities the term *fresher* is used.

the following message on Twitter: "Shouldn't say 'fishermen,' but 'fishers' sounds wrong as a gender-neutral alternative." Members of the governing Conservative party ridiculed McCarthy for suggesting that people should avoid the word *fishermen*: a senior Conservative MP, Charles Walker, declared that with such "meaningless utterances" McCarthy's party was "losing its mandate to be taken seriously."

The current controversy over *fisher* and *fisherman* has been going on for decades. The word *fisher* itself, though, goes back much farther than that, as anyone familiar with the 1611 King James version of the Bible will know:

> The fishers also shall mourn, and all they that cast angle into the brooks shall lament. (Isaiah 19.8)

> And Jesus, walking by the sea of Galilee, saw two brethren, Simon called Peter, and Andrew his brother, casting a net into the sea: for they were fishers. (Matthew 4.18)

It was not only in the Bible that fishers were to be found; analysis of surviving printed materials shows that the word *fisher* was used much more frequently than *fisherman* until the late seventeenth century. For a time both were commonly used—and then around 1750 *fisherman* started to be used with far greater frequency. Interestingly, this is not an isolated case: a similar pattern holds for *worker* and *workman*, with the latter beginning around 1750 to be much more widely used than the former. In the case of *worker* and *workman*, the twentieth and twenty-first centuries have brought a reversal: *worker* has again become much more widely used than *workman*. But the words *fisher* and *fisherman* have not followed the same pattern over the past century; resistance to *fisher* remains surprisingly strong, though T.A. Branch and D. Kleiber report that *fisher* overtook *fisherman* in frequency of use in scientific journals in 2013 and 2014.[1]

Is there in fact anything wrong with *fisher* as a gender-neutral alternative? It's a word that also names a small furry mammal, but those animals are not common and the context must surely almost always make clear that people fishing are not small furry mammals, and are not trying to catch them, either.

Fisher is not any longer or more difficult to say than *fisherman*; quite the reverse. We don't say *bakerman* or *farmerman* or *hunterman*. Why, then, are many people who are otherwise sympathetic to the cause of gender-neutral language reluctant to use *fisher*? In their respected guide to linguistic usage, Margery Fee and Janice McAlpine support Blair Shewchuk's argument that we should base our practice on the dominant practice of those in the industry:

> [The word] *fisher* has been resisted by the women and men who catch fish for a living. Blair Shewchuk, a language columnist for the CBC, offers this sensible recommendation: "… one logical conclusion is that *fisherman* is the right choice until women in the industry start calling themselves fishers."[2]

But if society had followed that logic consistently, we would surely still be calling garbage collectors *garbagemen*, police officers *policemen*, and fire fighters *firemen*; in none of those cases was it the workers in the professions who led the

---

1 . See "Should We Call Them *Fishers* or *Fishermen*?," *Fish and Fisheries*, 2015.
2   *Guide to Canadian English Usage*, 2015.

push for change. And in every case reasonable arguments were made that using a gender-neutral term would help to discourage society from seeing these professions as the "natural" preserve of men—and conversely, would encourage women to consider entering those lines of work.

Though defenders of *fisherman* make much of the fact that most women fish-workers say they prefer *fisherman* to *fisher*, they make little of the fact that there are very, very few women on commercial fishing boats, or the fact that there is considerable evidence worldwide of discrimination against women in the fishing industry. (In one recent case, Jane Tabor, a woman who was qualified to captain a fishing vessel but had been unable to obtain work recounted having been told that the "only place for women's breasts on a boat" should be "on the bow—as a figurehead.")[1]

From one angle it can be argued that certain "educated elites" shouldn't try to "impose" a gender-neutral term on an occupation when those actually working in that field prefer the gendered term. But from another angle, one might ask why fishing should be made an exception as society as a whole moves towards gender-neutral terms for occupations. Could it be that a certain other variety of "educated elite" is more inclined to think an exception appropriate in the case of a working-class occupation whose traditions have been frequently romanticized? (And in the other direction, might such an educated elite have fewer qualms about pressing for change in middle-class occupations, or working-class occupations in which traditions have never been romanticized—letter carriers, for

gender

---

1   See Jillian Kestler-D'Amours and Michelle McQuigge, "First Nations Woman Wins Discrimination Battle over Fishing Captain Licence," *The Star*, 6 May 2015.

example, or garbage collectors?) Interestingly, the strongest objections to using *fishers* rather than *fishermen* seem to have come not from women working in the industry but from people complaining to media outlets such as the CBC that the term *fishers* somehow grates on their ears.

Let's give the last word to two women who have fished as an occupation:

> "Fishing women don't really mind being called *fishermen*. I don't. In light of all of the serious issues we're dealing with right now, it's an issue for academics, but it's not really an issue for us. *Fisherwomen* would probably be a good start to give women the recognition they haven't been getting."
>
> –Mary DesRoches, Nova Scotia Women's FishNet, former fish harvester[1]

> [on why she has called herself a fisherman]: "Guess it seemed there were always so few of us [women.] *Fisherwomen* seemed contrived & awkward. I wasn't into making a statement."
>
> –Woman employed in the Hawaiian fishery, 2015 (as quoted in Branch and Kleiber)

This is one where there is plenty of room for discussion; what do you think?

Gendered Insults

The English language offers its speakers a slew of insults that work by associating the recipient with women's bodies

---

1   Quoted in "Women's Organizations Anchor Fishing Communities," *The Gulf of Maine Times*, vol. 1, no. 4, 1997.

and sexuality: words such as *twat*, *cunt*, and *pussy*. We have no objection to using these words to refer to the organs they describe (in any context where you think swearing is in itself appropriate; you may want to think twice before using them in your next academic essay). The problem arises when they are used to describe people—to insult women by reducing them to a single body part, or to try to insult men by comparing them to something feminine. If to call a man a *pussy* means to suggest that he is weak, cowardly, or oversensitive, it is hard to deny that the insult works because of misogynist ideas about women—especially when *dick*, for example, would insult him by suggesting the opposite, that he is insensitive or inconsiderate.[1] A related word, *bitch*, operates according to a similar principle: while a woman who is called a *bitch* is insulted by the comparison to a female dog in heat—a comparison implying that women are oversexed and not fully human—a man called the same thing is insulted even more by also being compared to a female human.

We think the case against anatomical insults can best be made in the context of those that attach misogynistic ideas to women's bodies. But what of men's bodies? If we call someone a *dick* or a *prick*, are we also perpetuating harmful ideas about masculinity? What about gender-neutral anatomical insults; is it all right to consider someone *a real asshole*? And what about insults in general; what, if any, place should they have in the ethical use of language?

---

1   See Melissa Grant, "5 Insults You Didn't Realize Were Gendered," *Bustle*, 26 February 2016.

gender

Slut: A Case Study

In their 2014 article "'Good Girls': Gender, Social Class, and Slut Discourse on Campus," sociologists Elizabeth Armstrong and Laura Hamilton found that, though plenty of university students call other students *sluts*, they have trouble describing what the term actually means. Does a certain number of partners, or way of dressing, or specific type of behavior make one a slut? Armstrong and Hamilton found that the students they interviewed were not able to provide any consistent definition of the word—but all of them were afraid of being labeled with it. One woman reflects on the way the word was used in her high school:

> "In my high school, ... you were a whore or a slut if you ate too much and didn't gain a pound. You were a whore or a slut if you bought the same prom dress as the head cheerleader. You were a whore or a slut if I don't like the way you look in that shirt, or I think your boobs are too big."[1]

The amorphous meaning of the word is part of its power. If there is no set of rules a woman can follow to avoid being called *slut*, then the word and its stigma can be attached to anyone—and *slut* becomes an effective tool for policing *all* women's behavior, and not just in the realm of sexuality.

Slut might not have a single, concrete meaning, but it has concrete consequences. The word reflects cultural ideas about rape that lead to women who are raped being blamed for being too sexual or too provocatively dressed. In 2011, for example, a Toronto police officer at a safety forum

---

1   Quoted in Leora Tanenbaum, *I Am Not a Slut: Slut-Shaming in the Age of the Internet*, HarperCollins, 2015.

caused a controversy when he advised that "women should avoid dressing like sluts in order not to be victimized."[1] And *slut* reflects a larger belief about the human value of women who are or seem too sexual—a belief reflected in *slut-shaming*, the practice especially common in North American high schools of identifying particular students as "sluts" and then bullying them, sometimes to the point of suicide.

In recent decades, some feminists have made an effort to combat these sorts of harmful ideas by reclaiming *slut*. In one landmark moment, in the early 1990s, feminist punk rocker Kathleen Hanna performed with the word written in lipstick on her stomach. And in 1997, Dossie Easton and Janet W. Hardy published their book *The Ethical Slut*, in which they proposed redefining the word to mean "a person of any gender who celebrates sexuality according to the radical proposition that sex is nice and pleasure is good for you." More recently, in 2011, activists were inspired by the above police officer's comments to begin an annual march making a stand against the use of slut discourse to blame rape victims. They called their marches "SlutWalks."

While some feminists have embraced the reclamation of *slut*, others argue that the word is simply too laden with ideological baggage—and with a long history of violence—to ever be reclaimed. Leora Tanenbaum, for example, argues that reclaiming the word is not a good feminist strategy given the way that women in contemporary western culture are "hypersexualized":

---

1   See Rick Madonik, "Cop Apologizes for 'Sluts' Remark at Law School," *Toronto Star*, 18 February 2011.

Reclamation of *slut* makes no sense for someone already assumed to be a *slut*. In fact, it may
be an act of self-harm; why denigrate yourself
even more than you're denigrated already? Why
deepen your own oppression?

For some feminists who advocate reclamation, however,
arguments such as these miss the point, which is that the
very attributes disparaged in the term *slut*—sexual freedom
and defiance—should be celebrated. A group of Seattle
SlutWalk organizers, for example, argues that

One of the most effective ways to fight hate is to
.disarm the derogatory terms employed by haters,
embracing them and giving them positive connotations. We feel that offering a place for women
... to self-identify as sluts does not disrespect
them—indeed, the disrespecting is done by ...
slut shamers who say or imply they are disgracing,
degrading, and dishonoring themselves.[1]

Other feminists concerned about positive uses of *slut*
point out that reclamation is easier for some women than
for others. Because of long-lived associations between
poverty, presumed uncleanness, and the *slut* label, reclaiming the word might be harder for low-income women, for
example; it might also be harder for lesbian, bisexual, and
transgender women, who face a greater threat of sexual
violence. And, as the activist group Black Women's Blueprint famously argued in an open letter to the organizers

---

1 Jessi Murray, Robin Sacks, and Samuel Schimel, "Our Response to the Conversation with Ross Reynolds' Coverage of Slutwalk Seattle on KUOW 94.9
FM," *Slutwalk Seattle*, 15 May 2011.

of SlutWalk, *slut* can be a particularly laden term for Black women in North America:

> In the United States, where slavery constructed Black female sexualities, Jim Crow kidnappings, rape and lynchings, gender misrepresentations, and more recently, where the Black female immigrant struggles combine, "slut" has different associations for Black women.... As Black women, we do not have the privilege or the space to call ourselves "slut" without validating the already historically entrenched ideology and recurring messages about what and who the Black woman is.[1]

Because the term cannot be disentangled from its history, Black Women's Blueprint argues, reclamation efforts do harm by giving the impression that its use is acceptable:

> [W]e are careful not to set a precedent for our young girls by giving them the message that we can self-identify as "sluts" when we're still working to annihilate the word "ho," which deriving from the word "hooker" or "whore" ... was meant to dehumanize.... [W]e do not want to encourage our young men, our Black fathers, sons and brothers to reinforce Black women's identities as "sluts" by normalizing the term on t-shirts, buttons, flyers and pamphlets.

For feminists committed to reclamation, however, the disparate impact the word has on particular groups of women is part of the reason why reclaiming *slut* is such a

---

1 "An Open Letter from Black Women to the SlutWalk," *The Huffington Post*, September 2011.

powerful gesture. The organization Global Women's Strike argues, in response to Black Women's Blueprint, that

> Women of color are among the most likely to be put down as "sluts," which is why we rejoice at SlutWalk embracing the word "slut" to remove the stigma; if we're all identified as sluts, that's the end of the insult which can divide us.[1]

Even for those of us who embrace the idea of reclaiming *slut*, it is almost never a good idea to use the word when referring to other people who have not explicitly identified themselves as such. So what word *should* be used when we want to describe someone who simply does enjoy sex with a large number of partners? One good option is *promiscuous*, a word that is gender neutral and does not imply an inherent value judgment to nearly the same extent as *slut* (used in the traditional way). *Promiscuous* also has the advantage of being an adjective, so it avoids reducing a whole individual to a single descriptor in the way that the noun *slut* can do.

But what if a person's promiscuous sexual practices actually *are* morally reprehensible? There simply aren't many gender-neutral words in English to describe this (though *licentious* might be a useful option, if it's not too stuffy for the occasion). One might argue, though, that a phrase will work better than a single word in these instances: *promiscuous cheater*, *promiscuous manipulator*, or *promiscuous liar* all have far more descriptive power than the amorphous *slut*. But whenever we're tempted to use language like this to describe somebody, it's also a good idea to question

gender

---

1 "Women of Color Respond to Black Women's Blueprint Attack on Slutwalk," *Global Women's Strike*, 2011.

whether promiscuity is really what's at issue—or whether by centering it in our moral judgments we're only perpetuating the same negative ideologies that underlie words such as *slut*. If someone is a cheater, a manipulator, or a liar, isn't *that* what we ought to be concerned about?

Tranny: Is It a Slur?

To many outside the LGBTQ community who want to be good allies, avoiding the word *tranny* seems like an obviously good choice—and, usually, it is. *Tranny* is often used as a particularly hostile and hateful slur, and many activists argue that it has become far too tainted by these negative connotations to be used under any circumstances. Since the possibility of verbal harassment escalating into physical violence is a serious threat to the lives of people who challenge gender norms, concern about slurs cannot be taken lightly.

But the trajectory of *tranny* is quite unusual; unlike most reclaimed words such as *queer* and *nigger*, which began with derogatory connotations and were later taken up by the groups they refer to, *tranny* first developed as a celebratory term and was then co-opted as a slur. According to theorist and gender-nonconformist Kate Bornstein, the word *tranny* originated among drag queens and male-to-female transsexuals as a unifying term that could describe both groups; ze is among those who argue that it should still be used as a celebratory umbrella term for "ANYONE who messes around w[ith] gender w[ith] little or no care as to how [that] might [a]ffect their standing in mainstream culture."[1]

---

1   See Kate Bornstein, "Who Are You Calling a Tranny?," 12 July 2009, and "Tranny, Revisited by Auntie Kate," 25 May 2014, *Kate Bornstein Is a Queer and Pleasant Danger*.

This unusual history means that, while *tranny* is being forbidden in mainstream media by activists who consider it unimaginably hurtful, it is still being used in a positive or neutral way by many LGBTQ people—just as it has been since the word first caught on in the early 1980s. *Tranny* is still used as an affectionate and/or complimentary term within some LGBTQ communities, and has long been used as a positive term of identity by many self-described trannies.[1] J. Bryan Lowder, writing for *Slate*, wonders if the condemnation of the word *tranny* by some trans activists reflects a conservative desire to distance transgender people as a whole from the more radical communities the word is associated with. He muses that "dismissing the deeply felt identities, histories, and understandings of others as 'offensive' somehow doesn't exactly feel progressive." A related issue is that the word *tranny* is commonly used in the sex industry—an association many transgender people understandably want to avoid, given the stigma sex work carries in western society. Bornstein argues against such capitulation to damaging prejudices, asserting that "[c]lassist sex negativity is no reason for me to cease celebrating my sex positive identity."

For people under the transgender umbrella, the decision to use or not use *tranny* must be made individually. For those outside the community, the best practice is much easier to discern: avoid using the word unless a group or individual makes it clear that they want to be described that way.

---

1   See Cristan Williams, "Tranny: An Evidence-Based Review," *The Transadvocate*, 28 April 2014; and J. Bryan Lowder, "The 'Tranny' Debate and Conservatism in the LGBTQ Movement," *Slate*, 30 May 2014.

Questions and Suggestions for Discussion

1. Using the *Oxford English Dictionary*, explore the meanings of and the etymology of *boyish* and *girlish*.

2. Using the *Oxford English Dictionary*, explore the etymology of *steward* and *stewardess*.

3. Using the Ngram viewer,[1] compare (and comment on) the frequency with which *flight attendant* and *stewardess* have been used over the past century.

4. Using the Ngram viewer, compare (and comment on) the frequency with which *mankind, humankind*, and *humanity* have been used since 1800.

5. Using the Ngram viewer, compare (and comment on) the frequency with which *office administrators* and *girls in the office* have been used.

6. Using the Ngram viewer, compare (and comment on) the frequency with which *salesman, salesperson*, and *sales representative* have been used since 1800. What word(s) would have been used for equivalent jobs in earlier eras?

7. Is *douchebag* a sexist insult? Why or why not?

---

1   For a quick introduction to the Ngram viewer, see the section entitled "How to Use This Book" at the beginning of the volume.

HUMANS & OTHER ANIMALS

Over the past two generations the ways in which humans treat other animals have become the subject of widespread discussion. But there has been scant attention paid to how changing attitudes should be reflected in English usage. In particular, the issue of what pronouns to use has until recently been little discussed—but it is arguably of considerable importance.

pronouns

No one nowadays thinks it odd to refer to a pet as *he* or *she*, but beyond that there is a great deal of inconsistency. At issue is not only *it* versus *he* or *she*, but also *who* and *whom* versus *that* and *which*. Should we say *the dog that lives next door* or *the dog who lives next door*? Should we say *the pig that plays a central role in* Charlotte's Web? Or *the pig who plays a central role in* Charlotte's Web? Should we say *the pig that they ate for dinner* or *the pig who* (or, more grammatically correctly, *whom*) *they ate for dinner*?

In contexts where non-human animals are portrayed as pets or as friendly and lovable, *who* seems to be quite accepted. *The cat who ...* and *the dog who ...* are commonly used, as are *the pig who ...* and *the cow who ...* in contexts such as children's stories. With dogs and cats *who* seems the more widely accepted alternative, even in negative contexts; Google shows "dogs who bite" occurring more than twice as frequently as "dogs that bite." Wild animals too we seem comfortable referring to as living creatures rather than things. In the case of the non-human animals many humans make a practice of eating, though, *it*, *that*, and *which* are used far more frequently. Should they be? Is a cow any more a thing than is a tail-wagging Labrador? Is a calf or a piglet any more a thing than is a kitten or a puppy? What about a shrimp? Or a clam? Where does one draw a line? For many people there may be no easy answers to such questions, but they are surely worth asking; as has often been the case in human history, debates over appropriate linguistic usage provide some of the most interesting windows into large ethical, political, and epistemological issues.

What should you do if you are writing of non-human animals? Treat them grammatically as things? Or treat them grammatically as sentient beings? To some extent the answer may be context-dependent. If you cannot tell whether the bird you see flashing by in the sky or the fish you see flashing by in the water is male or female, you are surely not likely to refer to the creature as he or she (though perhaps you might use they; see the discussion of they as a pronoun elsewhere in this book). But if you do know whether what you are looking at is male or female, is there any good reason to refer to that animal as it rather than he or she? Or to say that rather than who?

Try as we might, we can't see any. We have to acknowledge that the state of our language is still some distance away from any point where it would be frowned upon to refer to non-human animals as things—calves or chimpanzees, bears or bonobos, dogs or ducklings, hens or hippopotamuses. But we'd like to try to bring all of us, as human beings—human animals—closer to that point.

worth checking The cow that's pictured on that carton of milk looks a lot happier than the real cows that produce the milk.

revised   The cow who's pictured on that carton of milk looks a lot happier than the real cows who produce the milk.

Much as it may to some people seem forced or odd to refer to non-human animals in this way, English usage of this sort in fact represents a return to linguistic practice that was once well established. In 1865, for example, one Dr. Kidd recounted in the *Times* of London how he had saved a cow during the cattle plague of that year: "The men thought her dying ..."; "Determined not to give her up ..."; "little by little she revived." With "intensive" farming practices having become near universal in North America, most of us now have little or no contact with living cows and pigs and sheep and hens; no doubt it is not by coincidence that the growth of factory farming has been accompanied by a shift in the English language towards usages that encourage us to think of non-human animals as things rather than living creatures.

leaving the "other" out

Whether to say *who* or *which* is far from the only issue when it comes to how we refer to non-human animals. Let's look at a couple of other examples:

needs checking   Throughout human history, our understanding of animals and of our relationship to them has been debated.

needs checking   The way we view animals determines how we treat them.

To be correct, such sentences as these should also include the word *other*:

> *revised* Throughout human history, our under-
> standing of other animals and of our rela-
> tionship to them has been debated.

> *revised* The way we view other animals determines
> how we treat them.

This sort of error is clear to us in passages where humans are not one of the species being compared. Any editor who came across a sentence such as *The robin was flying higher than the birds* would think immediately *Wait—a robin is a bird—that's wrong,* and would correct it to *The robin was flying higher than the other birds.* But the human tendency to exaggerate the degree to which humans are different from the members of other species is so strong that in these contexts we forget that we are in fact a species of animal.

At some level, of course, we all know that the human species is a form of animal life—we are neither vegetables nor blocks of stone. Is it needless carping to suggest that we should acknowledge our animality in our habits of speaking and writing? Is it merely pedantic to insist that it's better to refer to *the way humans view other animals* rather than *the way humans view animals*?[1] Arguably, no more so than it is to suggest there is a problem with sentences such as *Slaves should never sleep in the same quarters as people,* or *The gestation period of man is nine months.*

1 For those well versed in the history of theory and criticism in literary studies over the past few decades, it may be easy to forget that, in the context of
everyday usages such as these, the word *other* signals inclusion. In literary
studies since the late 1980s "the other" (or, more frequently, "the Other," with
"Other" capitalized) has been used as a reference point for interpreting literary
works; in that context, the word *other* signals difference and exclusion.

humans &
other animals

As researchers long ago discovered, the way we use language both reflects and helps to shape our thinking. If we treated all non-human animals well, how we spoke of them might fairly be considered a matter of less seriousness. But the fact is that we don't; throughout the world non-human animals are horrifically mistreated; here in North America, over 99% of the meat and dairy products we consume comes from animals who spend their lives in conditions of extreme hardship in factory farms. The more we hang on to habits of speaking of (and thinking of) animals as creatures entirely different from ourselves, the easier it is for us to rationalize the cruelty that we condone.

Ironically enough, the two examples discussed at the beginning of this section ("Throughout human history ..." and "The way we treat animals ...") are both taken (slightly modified) from an excellent book called *The Inner World of Farm Animals*, which presents a wealth of research demonstrating that farm animals are far closer to humans in their intellectual and emotional capabilities than has commonly been assumed. Even those who are working to challenge the old stereotypes, in other words, sometimes use language that helps to reinforce them. It took us a long time to learn the importance of being careful about how we use *man*; no doubt the same will be true of *animals*.

the expression "non-human animals"

You may have noticed that this book often uses the term *non-human animals* in contexts where many people would say *animals* instead; should that be made a general practice? Where non-human animals are being referred to in the same breath as humans, we've seen that *other animals* is often an

humans &
other animals

appropriate term. But in many contexts *other animals* is not an option. In such cases we believe the term *non-human animals* to be appropriate in many contexts, purely on the grounds of accuracy: humans are animals, and so to say *animals* when we really mean *animals except humans* is often simply incorrect. And, we would argue, it can be harmfully misleading; as already discussed, if we gloss over what we have in common with other animals, we may be more likely to mistreat them.

As with so many other terms, though, context can make a real difference. Here are a few cases in point:

- For many centuries, scientists paid little attention to how animals think.

- Most philosophers now agree that animals should be accorded at least some legal rights— that they should not be treated merely as property.

- Unlike modern groups such as Mercy for Animals and the Humane Society of the United States, the nineteenth-century Vegetarian Society did not publish images of animal suffering.

The first statement is on a literal basis simply false as it stands. Using the noun *animals* in this context makes no allowance for the one exception to the generalization: through all those centuries scientists always made an exception for their own species—humans and how they think. Using the term *non-human animals* is one way to correct the mistake; others may also be worth considering:

- Until relatively recently, scientists paid little
  attention to how non-human animals think.

  or

- Except where their own species was concerned,
  scientists paid little attention until relatively
  recently to how animals think.

  or

- For many centuries, scientists paid little attention to how animals think (the human animal
  excepted).

The term *non-human animals* is similarly appropriate in the
second example; using that term acknowledges that some
animals—namely, human animals—are already accorded
legal rights.

- Most philosophers now agree that non-human
  animals should be accorded at least some legal
  rights—that they should not be treated merely
  as property.

In the third example above, on the other hand, it might be
argued that referring to *non-human animal suffering* could
reinforce the notion that there is a firm dividing line between
the suffering of humans and that of other animals. In a case
such as this, either alternative seems to us acceptable—but
we have a mild preference for the first:

- Unlike modern groups such as Mercy for Animals and the Humane Society of the United
  States, the nineteenth-century Vegetarian Society did not publish images of animal suffering.

- Unlike modern groups such as Mercy for Animals and the Humane Society of the United

States, the nineteenth-century Vegetarian Society did not publish images of non-human animal suffering.

Though we endorse the use of *non-human animals* in many contexts, not everyone does. Some object on the grounds of linguistic inelegance: if it is obvious from context when "all animals" and "all animals except humans" is meant, this argument goes, it is unnecessary to use a clunky phrase instead of a single word. Others object because they believe the phrase *non-human animals* is just as problematic as *animals* alone: the descriptor *non-human* establishes human beings as the standard by which all other animals are judged, focusing on what most animals aren't rather than on what they are. As Marla Rose of *The Vegan Street Blog* argues, most women wouldn't want to be called "non-male," and it's widely considered offensive to call a person of color "non-white"[1]—so perhaps the same logic applies here. On similar grounds, language expert Margery Fee uses the term *other-than-human* in preference to *non-human*. It's an argument that we think has much to recommend it—though in many sentences *other-than-human animals* may be a bit of a mouthful to say.

What do you think? Should we use the term *non-human animals*? Should we avoid using it (either on the grounds of verbal awkwardness or on the grounds that it might support rather than undermine speciesism)? Should we use *other-than-human animals* instead? Or should we use such terms only in certain contexts? The examples below may provide fodder for discussion.

---

1   See "Against Non-Human Animals: How Language Shapes Our Worldview," 11 February 2015.

humans &
other animals

- Every human finds the thought of eating other humans repugnant; human repugnance over the eating of animals is less universal—and more complicated.
- Do animals have a sense of the future? Many biologists now say that they do.
- Many animals have developed sophisticated means of communication.
- No animals were harmed in the making of this meal.
- He was acting like an animal.

other issues regarding human and non-human animals and the English language

There are plenty of other ways in which the English language reflects bias against non-human animals—and there is plenty of debate about how, if at all, the language needs to be changed in light of that fact. Andrew Linzey and Priscilla N. Cohn, editors of the *Journal of Animal Ethics*, opened the first issue of their journal with a series of recommendations for "avoid[ing] derogatory or colloquial language or nomenclature that disparages animals (or humans by association)." They were applauded by some for their attention to the ways in which our language can encourage harmful ways of thinking. Even though most non-human animals can't be insulted by the way we describe them, the way we think about them affects how we treat them—and they are certainly affected by our behavior toward them. But Linzey and Cohn were also mocked for what many commentators saw as going too far—for objecting to benign terms and proposing long-winded or inscrutable alternatives. Are the terms *pet* and *pet owner*, as Linzey and Cohn argue, demeaning to the animals we love and care for, and are *companion animal* and *human caregiver* better alternatives? (The authors of this book suggest that *human* may often be an attractive alternative to *owner*—as in "That dog over there—where's her human?") In some European jurisdictions and in the province of Quebec, non-human animals are now classed legally as sentient beings rather than as goods and cannot be considered property in quite the same way as one's television or one's footstool. Even in most of those jurisdictions, however, people do "own" their pets under the law, but does describing them this way encourage us to treat them as objects? Are *wild animals* better described as *free-living animals*, to avoid the connotations of "uncivilized, unrestrained, barbarous existence" carried by the term *wild*? Or is *wild* already sufficiently neutral, or *free-living* too unclear? Should we avoid common metaphors such as *sly as a fox*, *drunk as a skunk*, or *breeding like rabbits* because of the way in which they impose human traits upon other species? Or is such an extreme change unnecessary?

A CASE TO CONSIDER

What's Wrong with Billie?

What's wrong with the following passage?

> Consider [the case of] Billie, which got injured at the age of five. She was taken to South Australia for medical treatment, in the course of which she spent three weeks with [others like her].

The mistake seems obvious; even a child can recognize what's wrong with writing "Billie, which got injured...." Billie is in the next sentence identified as "she"; obviously the appropriate relative pronoun to use is *who* rather than *which*. Yet the passage above appeared late in 2015 in one of the world's most literate and carefully edited publications, *The Economist*. How could such a mistake not have been noticed?

The full context will help to make clear how even the most reputable publications may fall into such errors. The passage occurs in an essay on the degree to which research has been showing non-human animals to possess many of the sorts of sentience that were once thought to be the preserve of humans:

> Consider [the case of] Billie, a wild bottlenose dolphin which got injured in a lock at the age of five. She was taken to an aquarium in South Australia for medical treatment, in the course of which she spent three weeks with captive dolphins which had been taught various tricks.

Though Billie herself was never trained to perform tricks, she learned at least one trick—the tailwalk—by watching her neighbors, and then, once she was returned to the wild, taught it to several other dolphins:

> Billie seemed to have picked up [the trick] simply by watching her erstwhile pool mates perform. More striking yet, soon afterwards five other dolphins in her pod started to tailwalk, though the

behavior had no practical function and used up a lot of energy.[1]

If Billie is a *she*, why isn't she also a *who* rather than a *which*? Such a question is clearly not merely a matter of grammar. The reason inconsistencies such as this may be found in the language used by so many of us is that, at some level, many humans are unclear as to the status of non-human animals. Such confusion finds expression in this passage, in which it is implied that a non-human animal may be at the same time both a living, sentient, and gendered being *and* a creature of a much lower and less sentient order.

What do you think? Should we accept the inconsistency? Should we be consistent in one direction and refer to Billie as an *it*? Or should we be consistent in the other direction and refer to Billie as a dolphin *who* has learned the tailwalk and *who* has taught it to others? In that case, should we refer to all non-human animals in the same way? All mammals? All mammals and all birds? All vertebrates?

Questions and Suggestions for Discussion

1. Using the *Oxford English Dictionary*, explore the etymology of the word *cull*.

2. Using the Ngram viewer,[2] compare (and comment on) the frequency of use of the expressions *fellow creatures* and *humans and other animals* between 1750 and 2008.

---

1   "Animals Think, Therefore ...," *The Economist*, 19 December 2015–1 January 2016.

2   For a quick introduction to the Ngram viewer, see the section entitled "How to Use This Book" at the beginning of the volume.

3. Using the Ngram viewer, compare (and comment on) the frequency of use of the expression *had to put him down* between 1750 and 2008.

4. Using the Ngram viewer, compare (and comment on) the frequency of use of the expression *treated like animals* between 1750 and 2008.

5. Using the Ngram viewer, compare (and comment on) the relative frequency of use of the expressions *the dog that*, *the dog who*, *the fish that*, and *the fish who*.

RACE

When Joe Biden entered the bid to become the Democratic Party's nominee for the American presidency in 2007, he put his foot in his mouth right away by praising fellow-candidate Barack Obama; for the first time in American history, he suggested, a presidential race included a "mainstream" African American who was "articulate and bright and clean and a nice-looking guy." Biden quickly apologized for the remark and was forgiven by Obama, who made an effort to minimize the significance of Biden's gaffe ("We have got more important things to worry about. We have got Iraq. We have got health care. We have got energy. This is low on the list"). But he and millions of others nevertheless recognized the inappropriateness of what Biden had said. To understand why such comments are inappropriate, one has to explore what is implied as well as what is stated. "Articulate" is a long way from "eloquent"; it's a weak term of praise used particularly in situations where one doesn't expect someone to be able to speak well at all. If someone who looks as if they are very drunk starts to speak in perfect sentences, one might describe them as "surprisingly articulate." If one praises a candidate as an "articulate African American," one is thus implying that, among African Americans, the norm is to be inarticulate. And if one praises an African American for being "clean and nice-looking," one is again implying that such is not the norm. The depth of racial baggage that such phrasings carry may perhaps be better sensed if we imagine how they would sound applied to other people, or other groups. Imagine if Biden had said how good it was to have Hillary Clinton in the race because she was a mainstream white American who was articulate and bright and nice looking. Imagine if Barack Obama had described Hillary Clinton in that way.

Obama, of course, recognized that Joe Biden was no out-and-out racist—that while he may have had a few prejudices embedded in his habits of thought and of language, they were habits he was trying to change, and he was a person of fundamentally good character; less than a year and a half after Biden's unfortunate remarks, a victorious Obama chose Biden to be his vice presidential running mate. And the rest is history, so far as American presidential politics is concerned.

Unfortunately, vast and persistent inequality is also part of history across North America. And in both the United States and Canada, inequality is particularly pronounced when it comes to race. In the United States, Black and/or Hispanic Americans are almost three times as likely to live in poverty as are non-Hispanic white Americans.[1] In Canada, Black, Asian, and Latin American citizens are paid significantly less than white citizens, and are much more likely to be unemployed regardless of education level. For example, while in 2011 a white Canadian man with a full-time job made on average about $69,450 per year, the average salary of a Black Canadian man was about $51,653—and a Black Canadian woman's was almost $5,000 less than that.[2] But inequality in North America is not felt only in economic terms: a particularly alarming example is the incarceration level of Black American men, who are almost six times as

1   See Carmen DeNavas-Walt and Bernadette D. Proctor, "Income and Poverty in the United States: 2013," *United States Census Bureau*, 2014. This report finds that 9.7% of non-Hispanic white Americans meet the U.S. Census Bureau's definition of poverty, compared with 27.2 Black and 25.6 Hispanic Americans.

2   See Statistics Canada, "2011 National Household Survey: Data Tables," 2011.

likely as white American men to be incarcerated,[1] and who receive longer sentences than white Americans for the same crimes.[2] Canada, similarly, disproportionately incarcerates Aboriginal Canadians, who are ten times more likely to be imprisoned than other Canadians are.[3] Extreme levels of inequality also persist, of course, in many other countries as well.

Why is it important to know some of that background when you are thinking about language? Think of the case of a white student who is not accepted to Harvard Medical School, even though some Hispanic and African American applicants with somewhat lower marks were accepted; not infrequently you'll hear it claimed that this sort of result amounts to "racism" or "reverse racism" against whites and in favor of members of these or other minority groups. Is that in fact the case? Emphatically not. By definition, *racist* opinions or actions are founded on the core belief that the members of each race possess qualities that are characteristic of the race, and that on the basis of these characteristics some races can be classed as superior, others as inferior. Whatever the rights or wrongs of the policies followed by institutions such as the Harvard Medical School that do not base admission solely on marks, they are surely

---

1 See "Fact Sheet: Trends in U.S. Corrections," *The Sentencing Project*, 2015.

2 See William K. Sessions, III et al., "Demographic Differences in Federal Sentencing Practices: An Update of the Booker Report's Multivariate Regression Analysis," *United States Sentencing Commission*, 2010. Sessions et al. found that, with the type of crime and other variables controlled for, in the United States in 2008 and 2009 Black men received sentences 23.3% longer than white men. Many other racial and ethnic groups are subject to prejudice in the American justice system, but the treatment of Black men is the most extreme example.

3 See the Government of Canada, "Backgrounder: Aboriginal Offenders—A Critical Situation," *Office of the Correctional Investigator*, 2013.

not policies founded on a belief that one race is superior to another. They may be intended to create a campus environment more representative of society as a whole; they may be intended to take account of inequality of opportunity; they may be intended in some measure to redress other inequities. Whether such policies are appropriate or not, whether they are effective or not—these are legitimate questions to debate. But such policies are surely not based on a belief that whites are inferior and should be classed as such—and it is thus wrong to describe them as racist.

African American/black/Black

For the past two or three generations *black*[1] and, in the United States, *African American* have both been widely considered appropriate terms. The latter, of course, is only appropriate if one is referring to an American:

needs checking   Nelson Mandela is widely considered to have been the greatest leader of his generation—not just the greatest African American leader, but the greatest leader, period.

revised   Nelson Mandela is widely considered to have been the greatest leader of his generation—not just the greatest black leader, or the greatest African leader, but the greatest leader, period.

We know that it is correct to capitalize words that describe ethnicity or national origin, such as *Hispanic American*,

---

1   When used to describe North Americans, *Black* is sometimes capitalized; see the discussion later in this chapter.

African American, *Irish Canadian*, and so on. But what about *black* and *white*? According to the majority of style guides, these should not be capitalized because they describe skin color rather than nationality or ethnicity. According to this argument, a white or black person might be from anywhere, and a given person's ethnicity would not be accurately described as *white* or *black* but as, say, *Somali* or *Danish*.

As you may have noticed, however, *Black* is often capitalized in this book—often, but not always. The approach we have taken here is informed by persuasive arguments put forward in several quarters by those who point out that a large number of North Americans do in fact use *Black* as a term of ethnic identification—and for a very good reason. Whereas North Americans of, say, Italian or Irish background can readily explore their "pre-American" ethnic background, North Americans whose ancestors were slaves are simply unable to do so: they have no way of knowing if their ancestors came from (to pick only three of many examples, each with cultures at least as different one from another as are those of France and Spain and Italy) the Khassonke-speaking Khasso Empire in what is now Mali, the Yoruba-speaking Oyo Empire in what is now Nigeria, or the Asante-speaking Ashanti Kingdom in what is now Ghana.

Barrett Holms Pitner of *The Huffington Post* goes further, arguing that *Black*—with a capital B—is, in an American context, not only an acceptable term, but a term that should be used in preference to *African American*:

> "African American" fits within a narrative that implies that Blacks in America have a similar level

of connection to their ancestral countries as white Americans and other immigrant populations have. Many white Americans can name offhand the countries and even the cities that their ancestors came from, but Black Americans most likely cannot engage in this casual cultural recognition without paying for DNA testing.

By placing "African" before "American" we are implying that we have cultural roots predating the formation of the United States, much like white Americans and other American immigrant groups. We are telling everyone—including ourselves—that we have a foreign culture that is a better identifier than our American existence. Despite how badly many Blacks in America may want this to be true, unfortunately it is not the case for many of us, including me.[1]

Given that the history of slavery has deprived most Black North Americans of the connection to specific national roots that most other North Americans have, it seems to us entirely legitimate to choose the identifier *Black* as a primary descriptor of ethnicity. When *Black* is being used in this way, capitalization recognizes its legitimacy as an ethnicity—whereas not capitalizing it may be taken to implicitly disparage Black people and culture. As Lori L. Tharps bitingly notes in an opinion piece for *The New York Times*, the Associated Press stylebook

continues to insist on black with a lowercase b. Ironically, The Associated Press also decrees that

race

---

1   "The Discussion on Capitalizing the 'B' in 'Black' Continues," 24 November 2014.

the proper names of "nationalities, peoples, races, tribes" should be capitalized. What are Black people, then?[1]

W.E.B. Du Bois made a similar argument in the late 1920s, when *negro*, uncapitalized, was a widely accepted term:

> I regard the use of a small letter for the name of twelve million Americans and two hundred million human beings, as a personal insult.[2]

The New York Times and some other newspapers were eventually persuaded to alter their style guides and capitalize Negro—but this practice was not retained with the change in terminology to black.[3] Black is currently capitalized in many Black-focused journalistic publications, such as *Essence* and *Ebony*, and by many cultural critics—but not in many other places.

Should we capitalize *Black* at all times? Some argue that consistently capitalizing *Black* is a pragmatic approach, since it can sometimes be difficult to distinguish in practice between its use as a descriptor of skin color and its use as the proper name of an ethnic group. Of writers who use this approach, a few capitalize *White* as well, for the sake of symmetry. But *white* is often capitalized in the writings of white supremacists, and most writers rightly want to avoid any association with that ideology. Moreover, *white* simply doesn't serve as a primary ethnic identifier for any large group in the way that *Black* does in North America—or

---

1   "The Case for Black with a Capital B," 18 November 2014.
2   Letter to Franklin Henry Hooper, 14 February 1929, included in *The Correspondence of W.E.B. Du Bois: Selections, 1877–1934*, edited by Herbert Aptheker, U of Massachusetts P, 1973.
3   Also see Tharps's article for this and further information on the history of the capitalization of *Black* and of *Negro*.

race

indeed in any area where a history of slavery stripped large numbers of people of their original ethnic identity. (Conversely, in many parts of the world *black* implies nothing whatsoever as to culture or ethnicity; in Zambia virtually everyone has black skin, but the Bemba, Tonga, Kaonde, etc. all have different linguistic and cultural traditions.)

The approach we have taken in this book is to capitalize *Black* only when it really does refer to a distinct ethnic and cultural group, and not when it refers merely to skin color; we therefore refer to *Black Americans*, and count it correct to write that *in Brazil, Blacks and those describing themselves as mixed race now constitute a majority*. But we describe Nelson Mandela, a Xhosa born in South Africa, as *black*. We have not capitalized *white*, according to the same principle.

nigga/nigger

Almost everyone knows that *nigger* is a highly derogatory term that was once very widely used in North America; that the term conveyed a presumption that Black people were inferior to whites—and that the term was frequently employed as an expression of blatant hatred and contempt. In the mid-twentieth century the word *nigger* began to be acknowledged as racist and hence utterly unacceptable, and it disappeared from respectable publications and from polite conversation. But it never went away: the forbidden term continued to be used in certain less polite circles as an expression of racism—and it still continues to be so used today.

In the late twentieth century, as a gesture of resistance in the face of the continuing oppression of Black people in the United States, some groups of young African Americans began to "reclaim" the term *nigger* (or *nigga*) as their own, using it defiantly among themselves to refer to one another. That remains common practice today—and as a result, some young people of other backgrounds now sometimes wonder why they too shouldn't be allowed to use the "forbidden" term. The reason is simple: it remains tainted by the history of oppression with which it is associated. It is one thing for members of a group that has been on the receiving end of oppression to embrace such a term as an expression of solidarity. It is quite another for those belonging to other groups to presume to do the same.

American Indian/Native American in the United States

In the United States there is not broad agreement about what term is the most appropriate to use when one is speaking about indigenous people of the United States. The terms *Indian* and *American Indian* have long been condemned by some activists and cultural critics who argue that the term is a concrete example of the ignorance of colonizers; the name was first imposed by Christopher Columbus, who mistakenly believed he had reached eastern Asia. The word *Indian* has also, these critics argue, taken on negative connotations through centuries of American racism. In the mid-twentieth century *Native American* was proposed as an alternative—but many activists and critics have not embraced this new term. The term *Native American*, some point out, could apply to anyone born in America. For others, the history of oppression attached to the term *Indian* is a reason *not* to abandon it, as accepting a new name would help to sweep the history of oppression under the rug. As Christina Berry argues,

race

Native Americans did not suffer through countless trails of tears, disease, wars, and cultural annihilation—Indians did. The Native people today are Native Americans not Indians, therefore we do not need to feel guilty for the horrors of the past.[1]

Whichever term you choose to use, it is best, wherever possible, to refer to the specific tribe or nation of the individual or group you are talking about:

worth checking   Maria Tallchief, an American Indian dancer, was the first prima ballerina in the New York City Ballet.

revised   Maria Tallchief, an Osage dancer, was the first prima ballerina in the New York City Ballet.

worth checking   Sherman Alexie, an Indian from Washington State, has been a force in American literature since the early 1990s.

revised   Sherman Alexie, a member of the Spokane and Coeur d'Alene tribes in Washington State, has been a force in American literature since the early 1990s.

Indian/First Nations/Aboriginal in Canada

In Canada, it's not uncommon for some First Nations people to refer to one another informally or ironically as *Indians*. If you hear an Aboriginal person calling another Aboriginal

---

1   Quoted in Kathryn Walbert, "American Indian vs. Native American: A Note on Terminology," *Learn NC*, 2009.

person *Indian*, does that mean it's all right for every Canadian to do that? Emphatically not: many Canadians consider the term offensive—and with good reason. The word, which is inaccurate in origin (it derives from Christopher Columbus's mistaken belief that he had reached east Asia), has also been tainted by centuries of history in which those who had taken the land from the indigenous peoples used the word *Indian* to disparage those peoples. (One exception to the rule that one should not use *Indian* is discussion of individuals or groups who embrace the term because of the political rights it connotes; the word *Indian* is still used by the Canadian government to indicate *Indian status*.)

The most widely accepted terms used to refer to indigenous Canadians are *Aboriginal peoples* and, less often, *First Peoples*. Canada's Aboriginal peoples can be divided into three large groups—*First Nations, Inuit*, and *Métis*—and these terms should be used when you are referring to one group specifically. But be careful not to make the common mistake of using *First Nations* when you really mean *Aboriginal people* more generally:

needs checking   In the past decade, government policies have reflected a change in attitude toward First Nations rights in Canada, from the Far North to the Great Lakes.

revised   In the past decade, government policies have reflected a change in attitude toward Aboriginal rights in Canada, from the Far North to the Great Lakes.

race

Whenever you can, the best thing to do is refer to a specific tribe or nation:

worth checking   Neal McLeod is a First Nations painter, poet, and Indigenous Studies teacher.

revised   Neal McLeod is a Cree painter, poet, and Indigenous Studies teacher.

Eskimo/Inuit/Alaska Native

The term *Eskimo*, used to refer to certain aboriginal groups of northern Canada, Alaska, and other arctic regions, is considered offensive in Canada. If you are discussing the relevant group in Canada, *Inuit* is the correct word to use. In Alaska, however, the situation is more complicated because Alaska is home not only to Inuit peoples but also to the culturally related Yupik peoples, who can accurately be described as Eskimo but not as Inuit. Another, broader term in use in Alaska is *Alaska Native*, which includes not just Eskimo peoples but all indigenous groups in Alaska (including, for example, the Aleut). We recommend using the most specific term that makes sense in context. If you are speaking of all indigenous Alaskans, use *Alaska Native*; if you are speaking only of Eskimo peoples, use *Eskimo*; and if you are speaking of a specific group (or of an individual who belongs to a specific group), use the name of that group.

brown people

If it's acceptable to speak of black people (or Black people), why is it generally considered inappropriate to speak of *brown people*? There are many more people in the world whose skin color might best be described as brown than there are people whose skin color might best be described as black, or as white; if there were going to be a "default" color that we assumed humans to be unless specified otherwise, brown would have to be it. As discussed above in the context of *white*, of course, it's not appropriate to regard any particular color as a "default" that one assumes people to be unless specified otherwise. But there are other issues at play here as well. To understand them, it's important first of all to distinguish between particular individuals and larger groups. It may certainly be quite appropriate to describe a particular person as having brown skin—and in certain circumstances it may also be appropriate to refer to an individual as brown. The high school classmates of the daughter of one of the authors of this book, for example, would often distinguish between her and a close friend of hers by referring (with the full approval of both individuals) to *white Naomi* or *brown Naomi*.

That said, there are good reasons why expressions such as *brown people* should be avoided in most contexts, by most writers. One is the history of such expressions; in the nineteenth and early twentieth centuries, pseudo-scientific generalizations made by Europeans and North Americans divided humans into categories such as "the brown peoples," "the yellow peoples," "the black peoples," and "the white peoples," with the latter inevitably being assigned a higher status. The particular historical circumstances in which the term black came to be accepted by people of color in Europe and North America are touched on above. But no such circumstances apply for the terms brown people or yellow people. They remain as they were then: terms that are not generally endorsed by those being described, and terms that tend to flatten and to distort—to implicitly encourage those of different skin color to think of all brown people or all yellow people as more or less the same. In some cases individual people of color may wish to refer to themselves as brown. In some limited contexts, it *may* also be appropriate to refer to larger groups as brown—as in the following passage from a *New York Times* piece:

> The interests of the white working class have often been used by white political elites to stave off challenges to inequality and discrimination by black folk and other minority groups.... In the 1980s, Ronald Reagan appealed to disaffected white Democrats who resented being forced to share a small measure of the gains they had accumulated through bigotry and often official discrimination. Now we hear again the cry that the neglected white working class is the future of American progressive politics.... [T]he needs of the black and brown working classes, which are not exclusively urban, are, again, even in progressive quarters, all but forgotten.[1]

This passage occurs near the end of an op-ed piece on race and racism in America in the context of a Donald Trump presidency. The writer—a distinguished American sociologist of mixed-race background who identifies as African American—clearly wants to signal that the large group of "forgotten" members of the working class includes Hispanics, Filipinos, people of mixed-race, and members of various

race

---

1   Michael Eric Dyson, "What Donald Trump Doesn't Know about Black People," *The New York Times*, 17 December 2016.

other groups as well as African Americans; in the circumstances, "black and brown working classes" seems a serviceable short form. Dyson not infrequently uses such expressions when he is referring to people's skin color without reference to cultural background. (In the introduction to his 2016 book *The Black Presidency: Barack Obama and the Politics of Race in America*, for example, Dyson writes that "white and black folk, and brown and beige ones, too have had their views of race and politics turned topsy-turvy.") Given the historical background, though, writers should be extremely wary of using such expressions—especially if they are not themselves members of any of the groups such expressions might refer to.

Hispanic/Latino/Latina

Though the terms are often used interchangeably in practice, *Hispanic* and *Latino* have slightly different definitions. *Hispanic* describes people who are from or whose ancestors are from a predominantly Spanish-speaking culture or country—including Spain, as well as Mexico, parts of the Caribbean, and most Central American and South American countries (but not Brazil, where the dominant language is Portuguese). *Latino* (used for men and for groups of mixed or unknown gender)[1] and *Latina* (used for women) describe people who are from or whose ancestors are from any part of Latin America—meaning Mexico, parts of the Caribbean, and most Central American and South American countries, including Brazil.

---

1   Some argue that using *Latino* in reference to mixed-gender groups unduly emphasizes Latino men; the term *Latinx* (pronounced "lateen-ex") is sometimes used as a gender-inclusive alternative.

race

In reality, however, it is often not at all clear exactly which countries of origin are encompassed by either term; some Caribbean countries, such as Haiti, and some South American countries, such as Guyana (where English is the official language), are sometimes included and sometimes left out. The classification of the large population of Brazilian Americans is a particularly contentious issue. Some government agencies, such as the US Department of Transportation, treat *Hispanic* and *Latino* as equivalent and apply both to people with ancestry from any Central and South American countries, including Brazil. On the other hand, many—but by no means all—Brazilian Americans identify as neither Hispanic nor Latino, feeling that both terms should apply only to Spanish-speaking cultures.

A good deal of uncertainty surrounding the usage of *Hispanic* and *Latino* is to be expected, given that these terms represent efforts to group together such a wide range of people from such a very large geographic area. For this reason, many people who might be described as Hispanic or Latino prefer wherever possible to be identified more specifically—as *Argentine Americans*, *Cuban Americans*, and so on. According to a 2013 poll conducted by the Pew Research Center, this is the approach preferred by more than half of Hispanics and Latinos; the next most commonly preferred descriptor (preferred by 23 per cent of respondents) is *American*, with either *Hispanic* or *Latino* preferred by only 20 per cent of responders.[1] The broader markers *Latino* or *Hispanic* can be useful, however, because they acknowledge a shared history of colonialism, some shared cultural characteristics, and the existence of diverse,

race

---

1   See Hugo Lopez, "Hispanic Identity," *Pew Research Center*, 22 October 2013.

integrated Latino and Hispanic communities within the United States. As one Hispanic woman commented in a *New York Times* interview, "As Latin Americans, as Hispanics in the US, there's a community that gets built regardless of which specific country you're coming from."[1]

When it is appropriate to use *Hispanic* or *Latino*, is it better to use one term than the other? There is no consensus on this, and practices vary by region; in Texas, the most extreme example, *Hispanic* is almost always used and *Latino* rarely used. When a specific group's preference is unknown, it is fine to use either term, but when such a preference is known, it is of course best to use the preferred designation.

When using *Hispanic* and/or *Latino*, it is important to keep a few things in mind. One is that, though both terms are sometimes treated as racial identifiers, neither refers to race; Hispanics and Latinos can be Amerindian, white, Black, a combination, or anything else. It is also important to note that, though *Hispanic* refers to the Spanish language, not all Hispanics speak that language; many Hispanics whose families have lived in the United States for multiple generations do not speak any Spanish. And, finally, *Hispanic* and *Latino* are normally used in reference to populations in the United States (and, to a lesser extent, Canada); the general term typically used to describe people living in Latin America is *Latin Americans*.

Chicano/Chicana/Mexican-American

Some Mexican-Americans describe themselves as *Chicano* (the term used for men and groups of mixed or unknown gender) or *Chicana* (for women). The term is particularly

---

1   See Joe Brewster, Blair Foster, and Michèle Stephenson, "A Conversation with Latinos on Race," *The New York Times*, 29 February 2016.

likely to be embraced by activists who feel that neither "Mexican" nor "American" captures the distinctive culture of people with Mexican ancestry who live in the United States. In the past, however, *Chicano* was a negative term, and it is still considered offensive by some Mexican-Americans, so it should be used with caution. The best approach is to use whatever identifier the given person or group uses—be it *Chicano, Chicana, Mexican-American*, just *Mexican*, or just *American*. If the group or individual preference is unclear, however, it may be appropriate to use *Mexican-American*, which is the most common choice.

minorities/non-white people/people of color/ racialized people

Terms such as *racial minority, visible minority*, or simply *minority* are often used broadly to refer to all people who are subject to racial and ethnic discrimination in North America. While not everyone agrees that this term is outright offensive, it is often not the best choice. One reason is that the word arguably carries negative connotations of inferiority and unimportance. Another is that, when used as a synonym for "everyone except non-Hispanic white people," the word is often inaccurate; non-Hispanic whites may constitute the majority of the population of the United States and Canada right now, but do not constitute the majority of the world's population—or the majority of the population of, for example, California or Texas.[1] The silliness that arises when one uses *minority* unthinkingly in this way is exemplified by the opening line of an Associated Press news report on birth in America in 2011:

1 See Edward Schumacher-Matos, "On Race: The Relevance of Saying 'Minority,'" *NPR*, 29 August 2011.

> For the first time, minorities make up the majority
> of babies in the U.S.[1]

Another example is the oxymoron *majority-minority*, used to refer to areas of the United States where non-Hispanic whites do not constitute more than half of the population.

Certainly the word *minority* may still be a good choice in contexts where a specific population that really is a minority is meant—such as *Montreal's Haitian minority* or *Zimbabwe's white minority*. But too often *minority* is overused in a way that implies that racial disadvantage is a matter of numbers, when concerns faced by "minorities" are much more often a matter of discrimination than of population size. As journalist Joy Goh-Mah argues, the word *minority* carries with it "a very simplistic view of race relations, suggesting that discrimination only happens because we are a minority, and erases the fact that, even in countries where people of color are the majority, white supremacy and its effects are still very much present."[2]

A potential replacement for *minority* that we would also caution against is *non-white people*. This term can be tempting to use, since it seems to group together "everyone who doesn't experience the effects of white privilege." However, the phrase *non-white people* is often considered offensive because it posits whiteness as a standard that all other people are measured against.

Within North America, the most commonly accepted choice in situations where one might otherwise be tempted to use *minorities* or *non-white people* is *people of color*. Unlike

---

1   Quoted in Phuong Ly, "As People of Color Become a Majority, Is It Time for Journalists to Stop Using the Term 'Minorities'?," *Poynter*, 4 August 2011.
2   See "Part One: Ethnic Minority? No, Global Majority," *Media Diversified*, 23 January 2014.

minorities, *people of color* doesn't imply assumptions about population size, and unlike *non-white people*, *people of color* doesn't explicitly define people according to a characteristic they lack. Another, less common option is *racialized people*, a term often chosen to foreground the fact that race and racial discrimination are the product of social forces.

But even phrases such as *people of color* and *racialized people* are not without problems. Both involve grouping together non-Hispanic white people on the one hand, and everyone else on the other—a categorization that can imply that whiteness is a desired norm from which other people deviate. Such categorization can also mask differences among racial groups, when there are of course vast differences among the experiences of, for example, Japanese Americans, Native Americans, and Black Americans. As the journalist Janani asks,

> How do we, as politicized people of color, acknowledge the very limits of the term 'people of color' and the way it can mask our actual racial situations? For example, why do we keep using the phrase 'communities of color' [to refer to] targets of police and state violence when we primarily mean Black and Latino folks? ... Why are we afraid to point to the specificities of racism?[1]

There are, however, times when it really is useful and meaningful to group together all people who are subject to racial oppression in North America, as Joy Goh-Mah argues:

> [T]here was a time when I rejected the use of a blanket term to describe non-white people, seeing

race

---

1 "What's Wrong with the Term 'Person of Color,'" *BGD*, 20 March 2013.

it as an implication of our being a homogenous group, defined by whiteness, or rather, our lack of it. However ... I came to appreciate the term "people of color" as a mark of solidarity, an acknowledgment of shared oppression, and a call for unity against white supremacy.

Orientalism and Occidentalism

Readers will find "Oriental" on the list at the end of this book of terms to avoid. Why? "The Orient" was for centuries an acceptable short form combining geographical areas that are now referred to as "the Far East" and "the Middle East"— or by more specific names. Why the problem with the old name? In a now-famous book called *Orientalism* (1978), the literary and political scholar Edward Said set out to answer that question. As Said demonstrated conclusively, the term had come to embody a great many deeply rooted stereotypes. "Orientals" were regarded as exotic, inscrutable, less fully human than white Europeans, and mentally unsuited to the job of governing themselves; they were thought to be better off under the colonial rule of a Western power. Such views have underlain a great many of the actions of Western powers over several centuries—from the exertion of British colonial power in India and the Middle East in the nineteenth century to the approach taken by the American government of George W. Bush to Iraq. The term "Oriental" also, of course, had the effect of flattening difference. Use of the term reinforced the human tendency to see individuals from other groups as indistinguishable—and, in this case,[1]

1   "Don't they all look the same?" There is a seemingly universal human tendency to perceive the individual members of racial or ethnic groups one is unfamiliar with as all looking very similar. When I was working for (cont'd)

thereby reinforced racist views of those groups. If one uses a single patronizing umbrella term to group together a vast and diverse body of different cultures, one is spared the effort of learning about how those groups may differ one from another.

As Said and others have argued, the political dominance of the West has made Western prejudices disproportionately damaging—but the process by which humans form biases and prejudices of this sort is not, of course, one that happens only in the minds of Westerners. Ian Buruma and Avishai Margalit have pointed out that many critics of "the West" in Asia and elsewhere have conflated the United States with all of Western culture, have stereotyped this culture as coldly mechanistic and entirely oriented towards money, and, in extreme cases such as various jihadis, have come to regard the West and Westerners as "less than human, to be destroyed, as though ... a cancer."[1] Buruma and Margalit suggest that these extreme views may have originally taken root as the flip side of the attitudes that were being directed towards Asians by Westerners, and there is no doubt some

---

some years as a teacher in rural Zimbabwe, I was for an extended period one of only two white men for miles around—the other being Bernard Uters, a German doctor. I was thirtyish, slight of build, dark haired and clean shaven; Bernard was fortyish, muscular, blond, and bearded. We could hardly have looked more different—to anyone used to looking at white people and inter-acting with them. But many in the local community were not—and so it was that I would frequently be accosted in the marketplace by people calling me "Doctor" and hoping I would be able to help them.

As this example shows, the tendency to perceive the members of unfa-miliar groups as all appearing similar is not necessarily racist; those who called me "Doctor" clearly were not stereotyping all white people in any racist way. But it is nevertheless a tendency to be wary of (and to try actively to counteract as one becomes more familiar with members of other groups), for it can have truly pernicious effects if combined with various sorts of negative feeling. Such combinations are indeed a recipe for full-blown racism. [DL]

1   See Buruma and Margalit, *Occidentalism*, Atlantic, 2004.

truth to that. But regardless of how these prejudices originated, there can be no doubt that they are terribly damaging, that they operate in more than one direction, that they are often embedded in language—and that it is vitally important to do everything we can to counteract them.

Arguably "Africa" and "African" have taken on some of the same qualities that "the Orient" and "Oriental" once held for Westerners. Victorian writers such as the famous journalist and explorer Henry Morton Stanley (author of *In Darkest Africa*) helped to spread outrageous stereotypes about Africa, many of which are still with us in one form or another—as is the tendency to flatten distinctions among the many different parts of the continent and its many different cultures, reducing the continent to one amorphous mass. In reality, how much do the peoples of Morocco and Nigeria and the Sudan and Botswana have in common with each other? Certainly far less than do the people of the United States and Canada, or the people of France and Belgium. But we do not flatten Europeans in the same way as we do Africans; North Americans might speak of a vacation in Amsterdam or in Italy, but if they go on a vacation to Kenya they are likely to say they are going "to Africa."

Roma/gypsy

A few racial and cultural terms are so deeply encoded in the language that people may use them without being aware of their underlying meaning. One example of this is the word *gyp*, which originated in the stereotype that Roma people—often referred to as *gypsies*, though the term is now widely considered a slur—are congenital cheats. In North America, the "gypsy" stereotype is often imagined as a fictional or historical figure, but this stereotype does a great deal of harm to contemporary Romani people across North and South America, and especially in Europe. Both Amnesty International and the European Commission have censured the European Union for institutionalized discrimination against the Roma.

needs checking   I'm convinced that the shopkeeper tried to gyp me.

revised   I'm convinced that the shopkeeper tried to cheat me.

white

What's problematic about the term *white*?, readers may well ask. In fact it's a term that can be problematic from two angles. The first sort of problem occurs when it's presumed to be the default position. According to this way of thinking, white is normal; if you don't mention a person's color, then they must be white. It's often assumed, indeed, that white is a neutral tone—that white is almost not a color at all.

Entering the terms *white suspect* and *black suspect* into an Ngram viewer (which charts the written usage of given words or phrases over time) may help to make clear why it's problematic to think of *white* in this way. White people are of course far more numerous in North American society than are black people. The two groups make up roughly equal percentages of the American prison population.[1] Yet the

---

1   The fact that, within the United States, black people are incarcerated at a far higher rate than are white people is a widely discussed phenomenon. Kim Farbota provides a helpful summary of the discussion—and an informed opinion—in the *Huffington Post* blog post "Black Crime Rates: What Happens When Numbers Aren't Neutral," 2 September 2015, updated 2 September 2016.

race

term *black suspect* appears in print more than four times as frequently as does the term *white suspect*. Here, as in many other contexts, *white* is regarded by many people to be the default position, and therefore not deserving of mention. But it's not a harmless practice; if we mention *black* disproportionally in contexts such as this one, such habits cannot help but reinforce racist stereotypes as to black people being associated with crime.

But treating white as a "default" race is only one way in which people can fail to acknowledge the privilege whiteness carries in North America. As certain supporters of Donald Trump in the 2016 American election campaign brought out plainly, many white Americans regard their skin color as anything but neutral—and nor do they regard it as a marker of a group that has traditionally been privileged in American society. To the contrary, they regard it as a marker of a group that's deserving but that has been *under*privileged—despite all the statistics showing that, on average, white people in America enjoy far higher levels of income and of wealth than other groups. Averages can conceal a good deal, of course, and certainly some white people have not been at all privileged economically. Indeed, many working-class whites have seen their earnings decline during the twenty-first century, just as have many working class black people (and many working-class brown people). But a great deal of evidence also suggests that working class white people have suffered economically *despite* their skin color, while many working class black people and brown people have suffered economically in part *because of* discrimination on the basis of their skin color. Moreover, black and brown people are often disadvantaged in a variety of ways that don't relate to jobs or income and wealth levels—ways that a white people often find hard to imagine could happen to them. Laila Lalami made this point clearly in an article written just after the 2016 American election:

> If whiteness is no longer the default and is to be treated as an identity—even, soon, a "minority"— then perhaps it is time white people considered the disadvantages of being a race. The next time a white man bombs an abortion clinic or goes on a shooting rampage on a college campus, white people might have to be lectured on religious tolerance and called upon to denounce the violent extremists in their midst. The opioid epidemic in today's white communities could be treated the way we once treated the crack epidemic in black ones—not as a failure of the government to take care of its people but as a failure of the race. The fact that this has not happened, nor is it likely to, only serves as evidence that white Americans can still escape race.[1]

CASES TO CONSIDER

Name Calling: Woodrow Wilson as a Case Study

To what extent should we use the names of buildings, organizations, and so on to honor important people who have done bad things? No one is likely to name schools or museums or institutes after Adolf Hitler or Idi Amin, but what of historical figures whose record is much more

race

---

1   Laila Lalami, "The Identity Politics of Whiteness," *The New York Times Magazine*, 21 November 2016.

mixed? In 2015—a year in which race relations in the United States were particularly strained—the name of the Woodrow Wilson School of Public and International Affairs at Princeton became a hot button issue of this sort. Protests concerning the honor Princeton implicitly bestowed upon Wilson by naming the school after him (and, more generally, concerning the ways in which that university honors Woodrow Wilson) elicited an extraordinarily powerful response.

The essentials of the case were as follows: historical research has drawn attention to the prominent role Wilson played in purging the American civil service of African Americans (except from the most menial positions); in keeping any African American out of Princeton while he was president of that university; and in preventing the League of Nations from adopting a proposed racial equality principle when he was President of the United States. In response, some students at Princeton demanded that the Woodrow Wilson School of Public and International Affairs be renamed, and that a Princeton residence named in Wilson's honor also be renamed.

Predictably, many rushed to attack the students—and, just as predictably, many who did so shed more heat than light on the situation. Some declared vehemently that we must not try to "stamp out history"—as if the protesters were demanding that Wilson's legacy not be discussed, rather than demanding he cease to be singled out for special honors at the institution. As Karen Attiah rightly put it in a *Washington Post* column on this topic,

> Of course [such figures as Wilson and Cecil Rhodes] will never be erased from history; nor do

race

they need to be. But in forcing their sins into the international limelight, universities, and society by extension, must reevaluate the lionizing of such men.[1]

Others who attacked the students' demands emphasized the "nobody's perfect" argument—pointing to the public and private flaws in everyone from George Washington to Martin Luther King Jr., and suggesting that, by the protesters' logic, there is absolutely no one truly worth honoring.

While it is of course true that no one is without flaw, it is also true that, when we are judging public figures, large matters of public policy are more important than personal peccadilloes; that some have fewer flaws than others; that the achievements of some are greater than those of others; and, in the other direction, that the damage done by some is far greater than the damage done by others.

But how are we to judge fairly who should be honored and who is perhaps not so deserving of being honored? Another refrain of those attacking the Princeton students was that (to quote one comment in response to Attiah's column), people such as the Princeton students must "stop demanding that historical figures be judged by the standards of today rather than by those of their own time." One hears this said on almost every occasion when a historical figure is criticized for having been intolerant towards women, or towards those of other races, or towards other marginalized groups. The inference is often an extraordinarily simple one: that the past presents us with a flat picture, in which everyone in a given era (or at least every white male) was equally sexist, racist, homophobic, and otherwise prejudiced.

---

1   "Woodrow Wilson and Cecil Rhodes Must Fall," 25 November 2015.

Let's look at that assumption in the context of Woodrow Wilson's attitudes about race. Did other American presidents of the time take a similar approach in dealing with African Americans in the civil service? Did other Ivy League universities in the early twentieth century act in much the same way as Princeton did under Wilson when it came to admitting African Americans as students?

The answer is in both cases a resounding no. Grover Cleveland and Teddy Roosevelt don't have a great record when it comes to African Americans and the civil service, but Wilson's is considerably worse. In this respect, Wilson was worse as well than some of the oft-vilified Republican presidents of the 1920s; Calvin Coolidge, for example, had a relatively good record in this area. Wilson's racist policies as a university president during the years 1902–10 also stand in contrast to others of his own era. By the first decade of the twentieth century, African American students had been attending Harvard and Yale for more than twenty years, and were well established at Columbia as well. At Harvard, African American women students were attending in sufficient numbers that they founded their own sorority in the first decade of the twentieth century.

It is with reference to facts such as those rather than purely "by the standards of today" that we should read Wilson's refusal to allow even a single Black student to enter Princeton. "The whole temper and tradition of the place," he firmly declared of Princeton, "are such that no Negro has ever applied for admission, and it seems unlikely that the question will ever assume practical form."[1] Wilson made very sure that the question indeed did not "assume

---

1   Quoted in Keith Brown, "Princeton's Problem: President Woodrow Wilson's 'Racist' Legacy," *NJ.com*, 22 November 2015.

practical form" during his tenure as university president—and it was not until the late 1940s, some seventy years after African Americans had begun to graduate from Harvard and Yale, that the same began to happen at Princeton.

Historical figures in any given era are not, in fact, all equally sexist and racist and homophobic; the past is not flat, and we should not try to make it so. Nor should we feel obliged in perpetuity to pay special tribute to those who have been far more intolerant than others of their own era.

But in other ways, of course, Wilson was in many respects a force for good in America, and in the world. How to balance the two? It's a much less easy question than many have assumed. Even Anne-Marie Slaughter, a former dean of the Wilson School, who has said that she would once have found the idea of renaming the institution laughable, wrote in a 22 November 2015 Facebook post that she had come to consider the idea of renaming the school worthy at least of serious discussion.

What do you think? Should the name of this particular school at Princeton be changed? Is Princeton a special case, given Wilson's tenure as university president there? Should his name be similarly honored elsewhere? (There is a "Woodrow Wilson High School" in many an American city.) What about overseas: if an international peace organization wanted to honor Wilson by naming one of their buildings after him, would that be objectionable to the same degree?

race

"Black Lives Matter," "All Lives Matter"

The phrase "Black Lives Matter" and the movement associated with it has stirred an extraordinarily angry response from many whites—perhaps most prominently from white politicians associated with Donald Trump's presidential campaign. Among them is Trump advisor (and former New York mayor) Rudy Giuliani. Here is an excerpt from an 11 July 2016 CNN news report on his remarks:

> Former New York City Mayor Rudy Giuliani stood by his recent comments Monday that the Black Lives Matter movement is "inherently racist."
>
> "It's inherently racist because, number one, it divides us.... All lives matter: White lives, black lives, all lives," he told Fox News on Monday.

Just as extreme is the view of Newt Gingrich. Here is an excerpt from an interview with the Trump advisor (and former Republican Speaker of the House):

> Q: People would also say his campaign has been at the very least divisive and potentially bigoted. How would you respond to that?
>
> Gingrich: How can you be much more bigoted than Black Lives Matter?
>
> Q: I'm not sure what that means, actually. What do you mean by "much more bigoted than Black Lives Matter"?
>
> Gingrich: Well, [it's] a bunch of people walking around saying, "Black lives matter," who get pissed off if you say, "All lives matter."[1]

It's worth pausing to reflect for a moment on the extremity of these remarks. According to Gingrich, the Black Lives Matter movement rivals anything in history for its alleged

race

---

1   Joanna Slater, Interview with Newt Gingrich, *The Globe and Mail*, 30 September 2016.

bigotry—rivals the anti-black bigotry underlying lynching and slavery, rivals the anti-Semitic bigotry underlying the Holocaust. Such a view is self-evidently absurd—but is there a legitimate complaint hidden somewhere within the extreme rhetoric? What's wrong with saying "All lives matter"?

On the face of it, of course, nothing's wrong with such a bland and nearly indisputable claim; few people would argue that *not* all lives matter. The problem is with some white people's insistence that we should say "all lives matter" instead of "Black lives matter." The comments of Giuliani and Gingrich make clear that, when they hear the phrase "Black lives matter," they imagine another word to be there as well; they imagine that they are hearing "*only* Black lives matter." But no one is saying that; what is being said is that North American society, which has always tended to treat white lives as mattering more, has to be reminded that Black lives matter too—and matter just as much as do white lives. All this is very much a matter of context—the immediate twenty-first-century context (a movement begun through social media in 2013 when the hashtag #BlackLivesMatter was created in the wake of the acquittal of the man who had killed Trayvon Martin, an unarmed African American youth); but also the context of centuries of oppression for Black people in the Americas. The context, in short, is one in which all too often white mainstream society has acted as if Black lives didn't matter—or mattered a lot less than the lives of white folks.

John Halstead expresses well the problem with insisting that "all lives matter" in a piece that appeared in The Huffington Post:

race

[S]ome white people might say that singling out Black people's lives as mattering somehow means that white lives don't matter. Of course, that's silly. If you went to a Breast Cancer Awareness event, you wouldn't think that they were saying that other types of cancer don't matter. And you'd be shocked if someone showed up with a sign saying "Colon Cancer Matters" or chanting "All Cancer Patients Matter." So clearly, something else is prompting people to say "All Lives Matter" in response to "Black Lives Matter." ... [For many white people], there's something deeply discomfiting about the word "Black." I think it's because it reminds us of our whiteness and challenges our notion that race doesn't matter.... We were raised to believe that "colorblindness" was the ideal for whites. We were taught that we shouldn't "see color." And saying the word "Black" was an acknowledgment of the fact that we did "see color."

The problem with being "colorblind"—aside from the fact that we're not really—is that it is really a white privilege to be able to ignore race. White people like me have the luxury of not paying attention to race—white or black.... [W]hiteness is treated as the default in our society.

Black people, on the other hand, don't have the luxury of being "colorblind." They live in a culture which constantly reminds them of their Black-ness, which tells them in a million large and small ways that they are not as important as white people, that their lives actually do not matter as

race

much as white lives. Which is why saying "Black Lives Matter" is so important.[1]

One interesting suggestion regarding the phrase Black Lives Matter appeared in a 15 July 2015 letter to the Canadian newspaper *The Globe and Mail*:

> I wish Black Lives Matter would consider changing its name to Black Lives Matter, Too…. [That] would mean that they wouldn't have to constantly respond to those who feel the need to proclaim that "All Lives Matter" whenever they hear the organization's name.
>
> I, for one, would be very happy not to have to hear that sanctimonious platitude anymore.
>
> —Judy Minden, Toronto

Minden surely hits the mark when she terms "All lives matter" a sanctimonious platitude. But should the name of "Black Lives Matter" be changed as she suggests? Or does this suggestion somehow miss the point? In our view it does; to add the word "too" to the phrase "Black lives matter" would be to water down its powerful rhetorical impact; it could also be taken to imply that it's OK to treat black lives as some sort of add-on to the mainstream of society.

The authors of this book, then, oppose any suggestion that those in the Black Lives Matter movement should be expected to tone down the clear message embodied in the phrase "Black lives matter" simply because many whites

race

---

[1] John Halstead, "The Real Reason White People Say 'All Lives Matter,'" *The Huffington Post*, 25 July 2016.

have chosen to misconstrue that message. As Baratunde R. Thurston has written,

> some people ... have a well-intentioned but ultimately harmful point of view which says that any mention or acknowledgment of race is racist. That's not true. Some groups are subject to more acute and specific pain than others. It is not exclusionary to acknowledge this. It's simply honest.... The situation for Black people in the United States is and has for many generations been urgent. Our outcomes for health, education, wealth and more are far below what they should be. The compounding of these challenges with extra-judicial police killings adds gasoline to an already burning fire.[1]

Why, then, is it problematic to insist on saying "all lives matter" rather than "Black lives matter"? In short, because context matters.

What do you think? Can you think of contexts in which it would be appropriate to start movements similar to "Black Lives Matter" for other groups? Would it be appropriate to start a "Gay Lives Matter" movement in Uganda, where the lives of gays, lesbians, and bisexuals are under constant threat? Or a "Muslim Lives Matter" movement in Myanmar, where the Rohingya Muslim minority is oppressed by the Buddhist majority? Or an "Aboriginal People's Lives Matter" movement in Canada, where Aboriginal peoples continue to suffer from systemic discrimination by the white majority? Or, arguably, even a "White Lives Matter" movement in

---

1   Baratunde R. Thurston, "How Do You Feel about the BLM vs All Lives Matter Controversy?," *Quora*, 1 August 2016.

Zimbabwe, where the oppressive regime of Robert Mugabe is driving whites (as well as black dissidents) into exile?

Indians, Braves, Redskins

By the end of the nineteenth century almost every Native American culture was either under severe threat or had been wiped out. But images of the supposed fierceness and savagery of "Indian braves" still retained a strong hold on the imaginations of white Americans, and in the early twentieth century it began to be common for sports teams in American cities to draw on that imaginative legacy in a context in which it was desirable to have an image of strength and courage, even of fierceness. In baseball the Boston Braves (later the Milwaukee Braves, and later still the Atlanta Braves) acquired that name in 1912; Cleveland's baseball team was renamed the Indians in 1915; in football another Boston Braves team moved to Washington and became the Redskins in 1937.

For decades now many have argued—with good reason—that there's a strong case for changing team names of this sort, on the grounds that they stereotype Native Americans in one-dimensional fashion as fierce warriors. Arguably even more offensive are gestures such as the "tomahawk chop" of Atlanta Braves fans (along with its accompanying chant), or team mascots such as that pictured on the Cleveland Indians' logo, Chief Wahoo, with his tomahawk eyes and ludicrously demonic grin. Tara Houska, an Ojibwe lawyer, expresses the view of millions when she calls the image "a blatant racial caricature."[1]

race

I   As quoted by John Woodrow Cox, "Cleveland's Chief Wahoo: Why the Most Offensive Image in Sports Has Yet to Die," *The Washington Post*, 9 August 2016.

Many school and minor-league professional teams that formerly had names such as "Indians" and "Braves" have changed those names over the course of the past twenty years. But as yet no major league franchise has done so. Some claim that such a move would entail renouncing a long, proud tradition in local sports. But—to take Cleveland as an example—Chief Wahoo has been part of the Cleveland logo only since 1947. Even the name "Indians" does not date to the beginning of the franchise, which before 1915 was known successively as the Lakeshores, the Bluebirds, and the Blues. To rename the Cleveland team the Blues, say, would be no dishonor to the team's history—and, arguably, would pair well with football's Cleveland Browns.

The resistance to names that reference stereotypes of Native Americans has grown slowly but steadily. Toronto Blue Jays announcer Jerry Howarth was one of the first within the baseball world to become persuaded. Howarth has reported that he "stopped using team names like Indians and Braves and terms such as tomahawk chop and powwow on the mound after receiving a letter from an aboriginal fan after Toronto defeated Atlanta in the 1992 World Series." Howarth described the letter in an October 2016 interview:

> [It was] one of the best fan letters I've ever received. He said "Jerry, I appreciate your work but in the World Series, it was so offensive to have the tomahawk chop and to have people talk about the powwows on the mound, and then the Cleveland Indians logo, and the Washington Redskins." He just wrote it in such a loving, kind way.

race

> He said "I would really appreciate it if you would
> think about what you say with those teams."[1]

Howarth wrote in reply that he would indeed stop using
the offensive terms—and he hasn't used them since. More
and more baseball people are coming round to his point of
view—but many still resist change. And, much more surprisingly, so do many Native Americans. Few if any Native
Americans defend the use of the Chief Wahoo image by
Cleveland, but 90% of Native Americans surveyed by *The
Washington Post* on this issue responded that they were not
offended by the team name "Washington Redskins," while
70% of Native Americans reported that they did not find
the term "redskins" disrespectful to Native Americans in
any context:

> Across every demographic group, the vast major-
> ity of Native Americans say the team's name
> does not offend them, including 80 percent who
> identify as politically liberal, 85 percent of college
> graduates, 90 percent of those enrolled in a tribe,
> 90 percent of non-football fans and 91 percent of
> those between the ages of 18 and 39.[2]

Could this survey be flawed in some way? Might it be that
respondents to questions posed by a Washington newspaper were so keen not to give offence to the questioner
that they were reluctant to say that they found the name
of the Washington team offensive? Certainly when asked

race

---

1   Jerry Howarth. Interview with the Fan 590 radio station, as quoted in "Jays
    Broadcaster Doesn't Use Cleveland's Team Name," *The Globe and Mail*, 12
    October 2016.
2   John Woodrow Cox, Scott Clement, and Theresa Vargas, "New Poll Finds 9
    in 10 Native Americans Aren't Offended by Redskins Name," *The Washing-
    ton Post*, 19 May 2016.

what terms they themselves *prefer* to be called (rather than what terms they find offensive), Native Americans do not put *redskins* high on the list. But the survey has certainly given pause to those who had been confident that virtually all Native Americans would find the Washington team name offensive.

Many Native activists argue that, regardless of what the polls say, the use of names such as Redskins indoctrinates North Americans—including Native Americans themselves—to think poorly of American Indians: the article reporting on the poll results also quotes Oneida Nation representative Ray Halbritter and other activists arguing strenuously that the NFL should not "continue marketing, promoting, and profiting off of a dictionary-defined racial slur—one that tells people outside of our community to view us as mascots," and that can have a harmful effect on Native American children.

The authors of this book side with Halbritter and Howarth on this issue—but it's an interesting issue that deserves full discussion. Is it patronizing for those in the white majority to call for the team name "Redskins" to be dropped when a clear majority of Native Americans are evidently not offended by it? Or is the term offensive in itself, even if a majority of Native Americans are not offended by it?

A Special Case?

In discussions of team names, should the "Chicago Blackhawks" (or, as the team name was officially until 1986, "Black Hawks") be treated as a special case? Far from being an undifferentiated stereotype, the team name "Black Hawks" derives from a specific World War I military unit, the name of which was in turn derived from one of the most famous Native Americans—Black Hawk (or Ma-ka-tai-me-she-kia-kiak) of the Sauk Nation, whose 1833 autobiography has become a classic of Native American literature.

What do you think? Should this Chicago team name be treated as a special case? Or does the name "Blackhawks" still partake of some of the same stereotypes of Native Americans that so clearly are involved in names such as "Braves" and "Redskins"? The Sauk were forced from Illinois by white settlers; is it hypocritical for the descendants of those settlers to honor a Sauk historical figure now in that way? Or does that history make it all the more appropriate for fans of all backgrounds to pay homage now to a great leader of the past?

race

Questions and Suggestions for Discussion

1. Explore the etymology of (and discuss the appropriateness of) the following terms:
   a. All Blacks (New Zealand rugby team)
   b. "That's a black mark against him."
   c. "That's white of you."
   d. "It's only a white lie."
   e. black hats and white hats
   f. aborigine; aboriginal peoples
   g. black mood
   h. white bread (as a descriptor to mean *bland* or *uninteresting*)
   i. niggardly

2. The above case study "Indians, Braves, Redskins" reports the results of a survey that indicated as many as 90% of Native Americans may not be offended by the Washington football team's use of the term "Redskins." Discuss in this context whether use of a term that may not offend most members of the group in question may still cause harm.

3. The term African American first came to be widely used in the 1980s. Most African Americans now prefer that it not be hyphenated. Why? Explore the history of at least one other hyphenated term of this sort (*Italian-American*, *Irish-American*, etc.).

race

4. Using the Ngram viewer,[1] compare (and comment on) the frequency with which aborigine and aboriginal peoples have been used over the past century.

---

1   The Google Ngram Viewer searches the vast corpus of published works that Google has scanned (currently covering the period 1500–2008) for frequency of use. Once you have accessed the viewer, simply enter the term(s) you wish to check, separated by commas, then click "Search," and an "Ngram" chart will show you the historical changes in the frequency with which the term(s) have been used. The default historical graph provided will cover the period 1800–2000, but you can adjust the dates at the top left.

RELATIONSHIP STATUS

Mr./Ms./Miss/Mrs./Mx.

There has long been an inherent imbalance in English language honorifics, with *Mr.* used for adult males regardless of their marital status, but many people using *Miss* to refer to unmarried women and *Mrs.* to refer to women who are or have been married. In the early twentieth century an almost-forgotten seventeenth-century term, *Ms.*, was revived as an honorific that does not presume marital status. Whenever you do not know that an adult woman has expressed a preference for *Miss* or *Mrs.*, *Ms.* is the term to use (unless, of course, the appropriate honorific is *Dr.*, *Prof.*, etc.). The honorific for people of nonbinary gender is *Mx.* (usually pronounced *miks*).

partner/husband/wife/spouse

People who are married often presume that other couples are married as well; in fact, of course, many people have no wish to participate in the institution of marriage—or for a variety of other reasons decide that marriage is simply not for them. Unless you know that a couple is in fact married, it's best to avoid mention of their relationship status—or, if the context requires some reference, to use the word "partner" unless/until you are corrected.

With gay marriage now accepted through so much of the world, it's of course no longer appropriate to assume that a man's spouse will be his wife, or that a woman's spouse will be her husband.

Questions and Suggestions for Discussion

1. Using the *Oxford English Dictionary*, explore the etymology of the expressions *common law marriage* and *living in sin*. As well, using the Ngram viewer,[1] check (and comment on) the historical patterns as to frequency of use of these terms through to 2008. Why would use of the term *common law marriage* have increased so steeply in the early 2000s? Why would use of the term *living in sin* not have declined more dramatically?

2. Using the *Oxford English Dictionary*, explore the etymology of the word *bastard*.

3. Use the *Oxford English Dictionary* to explore the use of the word *Master* as an honorific used to refer to young males of wealthy or aristocratic backgrounds.

4. Using the Ngram viewer, compare (and comment on) the frequency with which the expression *illegitimate child* was used from 1750 through 2008.

---

[1] For a quick introduction to the Ngram viewer, see the section entitled "How to Use This Book" at the beginning of the volume.

RELIGION

It is never acceptable to use religious slurs such as *Bible thumper*, *fundie*, *towelhead*, *infidel*, or *heathen*—no matter how strongly you disagree with a given group's beliefs or actions. (One exception is the term *pagan*, which has been adopted by some Neopagan groups but is considered offensive when used to describe anyone else.) But inclusive language regarding religion requires more than avoiding a list of derogatory words. One important guideline is to avoid language that implies an expectation that everyone shares your beliefs and practices. This is especially important if you practice the dominant religion in the place where you live (for example, if you are a Christian in North America or Europe). We can surely agree it's important to be thoughtful about situations where our language might impose our religious beliefs (or lack thereof) on others, but it can be difficult to tell what we really ought to say or not say, and what guidelines are unnecessarily restrictive. If an atheist is in the hospital, is it rude for his theistic friend to tell him he will be *in her prayers* rather than *in her thoughts*? Is it offensive for a Christian to say *Happy Easter* to a stranger whose religion he does not know? Is it offensive for the same Christian to say *Happy Easter* to a stranger who is in line at the grocery store with a basket full of eggs and food coloring? Would the school closure in late December and early January be more accurately described as *Christmas Holiday* or as *Winter Break*? When an atheist sneezes, should anyone say *bless you*? The answers to some of these questions are more trivial than others; all of them suggest something about how we relate to people with beliefs that differ from our own.

anti-Semitism

Given the generally high level of awareness in Western society of the evils of anti-Semitism, it is extraordinary that *jew* is still sometimes used in casual conversation as a verb in the same way that *gyp* is used—and that *Jewish* can still sometimes be encountered as a synonym for *stingy*. These are usages that have their roots in a long tradition of anti-Jewish prejudice in the many centuries during which most Christian societies prohibited Jews from entering most respectable occupations, leaving Jews little choice but to provide services such as moneylending that Christians needed but for various reasons did not want to provide themselves. Moneylending then became part of the vicious stereotyping that surrounded Jews. Like other extremely offensive terms discussed in this book, terms that preserve old anti-Semitic prejudices should never be allowed to go unchallenged. When they are challenged, speakers will often realize they have been unthinkingly using a coinage learnt in childhood—and will change.

A more subtle form of anti-Semitism finds expression in references to Jewish people's religious or ethnic affiliation where such information is not relevant; the effect, of course, is often to reinforce old stereotypes.

worth checking In 1961 the Canadian government appointed Louis Rasminsky, a Jew who had worked at the Bank of Canada for over twenty years, as Governor of the bank.

revised In 1961 the Canadian government appointed Louis Rasminsky, who had worked at the Bank of Canada for over twenty years, as Governor of the bank.

In this context Rasminsky's religion is obviously not relevant. If, however, the subject is the demographic make-up of the Canadian civil service establishment in the 1950s and 1960s, mentioning Rasminsky's religious background would be entirely appropriate:

> In the 1950s and early 1960s, the Canadian civil service was still very much dominated by white males, almost all of them of Christian background. Louis Rasminsky, a Jew who served as Deputy Governor and then as Governor of the Bank of Canada during this period, was one of very few exceptions.

religious extremism

A difficult issue is how to refer to extremists affiliated with a particular religion. Should those who profess faith in Islam but believe it is acceptable for them to kill and maim vast numbers of civilians who are associated with organizations they despise (Osama bin Laden's followers killing 2,996 people on September 11, 2001, or followers of the Islamic State movement killing thousands in Iraq and Syria in 2014, for example) be called Islamic fundamentalists, or Islamists, or jihadis, or terrorists, or simply mass killers? If someone claims to be following the Islamic faith and commits extreme acts of horrendous violence against unarmed civilians in the name of religion, many argue that it's entirely fair to describe that person as an Islamic extremist. But fair to whom? When the two words are brought together, inevitably something of the one rubs off on the other, leaving some suggestion in the minds of those reading or hearing the term that extremism comes naturally to Muslims. Many North Americans may appreciate this point more clearly if we think of the phrase *Christian extremist*—a term one hears much less often than *Islamic Extremist*. Does it seem appropriate to use that term to describe the shooter who killed three people at a Colorado Planned Parenthood clinic in 2015, and who professed extreme views regarding abortion and his Christian faith? Probably not: a strong argument can be made that no religion deserves to be identified through the actions of its most violent adherents.

The best way to approach such questions may be to be as specific as possible—and to try to use language that cannot be taken to equate the beliefs of an entire religious group with those of extremists on the fringes of that religion.

worth checking — Hindu terrorists killed over a thousand Muslims in the violence in India's Gujarat state in 2002.

revised — Extremists believed to be associated with the Vishva Hindu Parishadm (VHP) killed over a thousand Muslims in the violence in India's Gujarat state in 2002.

Much as one should be careful in choosing one's words in such cases, one should also strive to be direct where the facts are plain, or where the weight of probability points clearly to a particular conclusion.

worth checking — Extremists believed to be associated with the Vishva Hindu Parishadm (VHP) killed over a thousand Muslims in the "communal violence" in India's Gujarat state in 2002. Some have claimed that the state police and the Gujarat state government were complicit in the violence; it has been alleged that the police and the Gujarat state government (led by Narenda Modi, now Prime Minister of all of India) did little or nothing to stop the massacres or to prosecute the perpetrators, and some have suggested that Modi's government helped to plan the targeted attacks on Muslims.

[Though Modi and others deny it, Human Rights Watch and other impartial organizations have all concluded that the police and Gujarat state government facilitated the killings. What remains to some degree uncertain is whether or not they helped plan the attacks. In such cases responsible writers give their readers a sense of the weight of probability, rather than retreating retreat into a "he said/she said" form of obfuscation.]

revised Extremists believed to be associated with the Vishva Hindu Parishadm (VHP) killed over a thousand Muslims in the "communal violence" in India's Gujarat state in 2002. A strong body of evidence suggests that the state police and the Gujarat state government were complicit in the violence; the police and the Gujarat state government (led by Narenda Modi, now Prime Minister of all of India) did little or nothing to stop the massacres or to prosecute the perpetrators, and reputable sources have claimed that Modi's government helped to plan the targeted attacks on Muslims.

The term *radical Islam* was bandied about very freely during the 2016 American presidential campaign, with Republican candidate Donald Trump accusing Democratic candidate Hillary Clinton of being "afraid" to use the term.

As with many other issues, it's important to try to separate understandable repugnance for the bullying style with which this accusation was delivered from the underlying issue itself—whether or not it is appropriate to use the term *radical Islam*. Groups such as ISIS/ISIL and Al-Qaeda are indeed radical, and they do indeed represent certain strands of Islam. Why, then, should we not refer to them as representing radical Islam? Isn't that just calling a spade a spade?

No, is the short answer. And the reason is simple: such phrases work to create an ambiguity that fosters the impression that the religion as a whole is radical, or that the actions of radicals in some way reflect the beliefs of moderate members of the religion. Imagine calling those Christians who call for gays to be sentenced to death representatives of radical Christianity. Or those Buddhists who would like to exterminate Muslims in Burma and Sri Lanka representatives of radical Buddhism. Such phrases can readily suggest that Islam, or Christianity, or Buddhism, or whatever religion is being named, is by its very nature radical—and that any member of that religion is prone to extremism.

That is of course very much the impression of Islam that Trump's many diatribes left in people's minds during the 2016 campaign. And it has no basis whatsoever in fact. Though extremists are to be found in every religion—and though the extremists that may be found today in certain strands of Islam currently pose a very serious danger—the overall history of Islam is no more one of extremism and violence than is the history of Christianity. The overwhelming majority of Muslims in the world today are peaceful—and far from radical. Using a phrase such as *radical Islam*, then, has the effect of associating all members of the religion with the actions and ideology of a small minority. The effect of such rhetoric is to mislead non-Muslims as to the attitudes of most Muslims—and to make North America even more unfriendly to ordinary practitioners of Islam, which can only help the cause of radical groups.

CASES TO CONSIDER

"Islamist" and the "So-Called Islamic State"

With some justification, it's frequently argued that we should avoid using terms such as "Islamists" when we are speaking of groups advocating the violent suppression of all other religious belief, on the grounds that such terms tend to associate the entire faith in all its many branches with the beliefs and actions of a tiny minority. Would it be judged acceptable to give the name *Christianists* to a small group of Christians advocating the violent suppression of other religions—and of moderate Christianity? Not likely.

It seems clear that we should not impose from the outside a term like *Islamist*. But what if a violent minority are trying to name *themselves* in a way that implies their view is (or should be) the stance of the religion as a whole? Such is the case with the term *Islamic State*. In most cases there is much to be said for the principle of referring to groups in the way that they themselves prefer to be referred to, but, in the case of *Islamic State*, should we honor this principle? Or should we, as do many who oppose the group, refer to

religion

them as members of *DAESH* or *DA'ISH*, an acronym of the group's former full name ("al-Dawla al-Islamiya al-Iraq al-Sham," or "Islamic State of Iraq and the Levant")? Muslims who do not subscribe to the ideology of IS/DAESH—which is to say, the vast majority of Muslims, living not only in countries oppressed by IS/DAESH but also across the rest of the world—naturally have a keen interest in preventing it from establishing itself as representative of Islam or as a legitimate state. But is using *DAESH* glossing over the important role that religious extremism in fact plays in the organization's ideology? And regardless of how we feel about the Islamic State's actions, is it simply petty, and potentially confusing, to reject a group's own self-defined term and replace it with an insulting one? In Arabic *DAESH* is very close in sound to the words for "someone who squashes something underfoot" (*daes*) and for "someone who causes trouble" (*dahes*). Referring to the group as *DAESH*, then, is a little like referring to the Committee to Re-elect the President as *CREEP* (as many opponents of Richard Nixon delighted in doing in 1972).

A third approach is to use a phrase such as *so-called Islamic State* so as to indicate that one does not accept the legitimacy of the group to speak for Islam (or, perhaps, its political legitimacy).

Which is most appropriate?

And what of other, parallel situations? If a political party in a European country called the Christian Democratic Party started to adopt extremist positions and advocate the forced conversion or killing of non-Christians and moderate Christians, should they still be referred to as *the Christian Democratic Party* in that country? Or should those resisting their version of Christianity start referring to them as *the so-called Christian Democratic Party*? What about historical events; should we refer to *so-called Christians* massacring heretics in the Middle Ages?

Anti-Semitism and Anti-Judaism: Are They the Same? What about Anti-Zionism? Is Anti-Zionism Merely Anti-Semitism in Disguise?

Unlike terms such as *anti-Christian* and *Islamophobic*, which explicitly refer to people as categorized by religion, the term predominantly used to denote prejudice against Jews specifies a racial and linguistic category—Semitic—rather than a religious one. Though terms such as *Semitic peoples* are no longer used in modern systems of classification, the habit persists of thinking of Jews as a racial as well as a cultural and religious group.

The term *anti-Judaism* has long been available as an alternative to *anti-Semitism*, and in practice, the two are generally used interchangeably. Some, however, draw a fine distinction between *anti-Judaism* as a prejudice against the Jewish religion—one that is usually motivated by the prejudiced person's own religious beliefs—and *anti-Semitism* as a politically motivated prejudice against Jewish culture and/or ethnicity.

But what about *anti-Zionism*—is it an equivalent to *anti-Semitism*? So far as the plain meaning of the terms is concerned, the answer to that question has to be *no*. The territory now controlled by Israel has been contested for millennia; reasonable claims can be made on historical and religious grounds that it is rightly the "homeland" of several peoples. In the early twentieth century relatively few Jews lived in what is now Israel—but Jews had been displaced from many other parts of the world and were in danger of being displaced from others. Many began to call for a Jewish homeland to be established in a part of the Middle East to which Judaism had strong historic and cultural ties. The term *Zionism* was originally applied to the movement striving to create such a Jewish homeland. Understandably, Zionism gained considerable momentum in the wake of the Holocaust; with 6 million Jews having been murdered and many more displaced during World War II, many saw the case for a Jewish homeland in a new and more favorable light. Once such a homeland—the state of Israel—was established (in 1949), Zionism became a movement to *preserve* the existence of that state, based on the same principles. *Anti-Zionism* is the movement in opposition to Israel's enactment of those principles; some anti-Zionists continue to oppose the existence of Israel as a separate nation-state, while others oppose its existence as a nation-state with a religious identity. More moderate anti-Zionists support the existence of Israel but argue that it must cede land to Palestinians so as to also make a Palestinian homeland possible. Anti-Zionists generally point to the inadequate provisions made in 1949 for the Palestinians displaced by the creation of the State of Israel. And they point as well to the ill-treatment of Palestinians at Israeli hands since 1949—most notably, to the appalling conditions that Palestinians in the Gaza strip and the West Bank territories have often been subjected to.

Much as Israel is a state strongly associated with Judaism, many Jews have joined non-Jews in opposing Israel's actions toward Palestinians, while many non-Jews as well as Jews consider Israel's actions to be justified; in other

religion

words, many non-Jews are Zionists and many Jews are anti-Zionists. (In somewhat similar fashion, it might be pointed out, many of the Shi'a branch of Islam have opposed the various repressive actions towards non-Shi'a Muslims that the state of Iran has enacted during the period it has been the self-declared homeland of that branch of the Islamic religion.)

Anti-Zionism and anti-Semitism are thus clearly quite different things; to be against Israel (or to criticize actions taken by Israel) is not necessarily to be against Jews. But is there then no basis whatsoever for the suggestion that anti-Zionism and anti-Semitism are sometimes linked? Sadly, there is indeed such a basis. When some extreme anti-Semites in America (David Duke, for example) rail against Zionism, they see the actions of Israel as connected to "the Jewish war on Christmas," "the Jewish extremist takeover of America," and "Jewish Supremacist control of our society, mass media, financial institutions and government." To any thinking person, such views are ludicrous. But the habit of using anti-Zionism to express anti-Jewish feeling can sometimes be found much closer to the mainstream of North American opinion. Indeed, it is hard not to believe that anti-Semitism fuels at least some of the anti-Israel sentiment around the globe, from both left-wing and right-wing sources: one does not need to be a defender of Israel's behavior towards the Palestinians to see an imbalance in the fact that the United Nations condemns human rights violations by the Israeli government with far, far greater frequency than it does those of any other nation on earth.

Is anti-Zionism always merely anti-Semitism in disguise? No. But is anti-Zionism *sometimes* fueled by anti-Semitism? Sometimes, yes, it probably is.

Here are some questions for discussion:

- Should we use the term *anti-Judaism* in preference to the term *anti-Semitism*?
- To what extent is the idea of founding a nation
  state on religious principles problematic?
  Should all nation-states strive to keep religion
  and politics entirely separate?
- To what extent is religious prejudice (whether
  anti-Judaism, anti-Islam, or of any other sort)
  rooted in the same soil as racial prejudice? As
  class prejudice? As prejudice on the basis of
  gender or sexual orientation?

A Happy Holiday?

Western countries became more and more aware of multi-
culturalism in the late twentieth century—and many people
started to notice when it came time to send out Christmas cards for their organization that not everyone on the
list celebrated Christmas. People noticed too that many
faiths celebrated holidays other than Christmas at about
the same time. Soon *Season's Greetings* and *Happy Holidays*
became common alternatives to *Merry Christmas* on cards
and on storefront signs. And some people started to say
"Have a happy holiday!" to their colleagues as they left the
office.

How did we get from there to the supposed "war on
Christmas" that began to preoccupy various conservative
commentators in the early twenty-first century? "Who
are these politically correct killjoys who think you can't
say Merry Christmas just because someone of a different religion might be in the room?" thundered a *Toronto*

Sun editorial.[1] "Now they are trying to abolish Christmas," fumed columnist Peter Hitchens in the *Daily Mail*.[2]

The truth is that there never was any "war on Christmas"; there was only a war by "defenders of Christmas" against an imagined enemy. Who actually asserted that Christians shouldn't say *Merry Christmas* if "someone of a different religion might be in the room"? No one. That was the view that the *Toronto Sun* imagined would be held by the 49% of respondents to a Public Religion Research Institute poll which asked the following question:

> Do you think stores and businesses should greet customers with "Happy Holidays" or "Season's Greetings" instead of "Merry Christmas," out of respect for people of different faiths, or not?

The question was not "Should stores and businesses be *forbidden* to use 'Merry Christmas' as a greeting?" And the question was certainly not "Should individuals be told they can't say 'Merry Christmas' if someone of a different religion is in the room?"

But self-styled defenders of Christmas can point to many other indications of the war that's being waged against Christmas. In 2015, for example, Starbucks chose not to print any written greeting on their seasonal coffee cups, and simply color them a festive red.[3] It's hard to imagine a nastier attack.

An Ngram showing the frequency of use of the terms *Merry Christmas*, *Season's Greetings*, and *Happy Holidays* over the period 1800 to 2015 shows some interesting results.

---

1   Anonymous, "Saying 'Merry Christmas' with Pride," 24 December 2013.
2   "A Merry Christmas: Before It's Abolished," 22 December 2002.
3   They still, however, offered their seasonal "Christmas blend."

First of all, *Merry Christmas* has always been used several times more frequently than the two other greetings combined. And the pattern since 2000 or thereabouts (when the "war on Christmas" is alleged to have begun)? The difference has widened; in 2015 *Merry Christmas* was used roughly seven times more frequently than the runner up, *Happy Holidays*.

It would appear that what many of the defenders of Christmas are truly angry about is inclusivity. Of course it just doesn't sound great to say "I'm against inclusivity"; how much more satisfying it is to imagine a war and proudly style oneself as fighting "against political correctness" and as "a defender of Christmas."

Questions and Suggestions for Discussion

1. Expressions such as *international financial conspiracy* and *globalist cabal* are often used as code, suggesting anti-Semitic views without stating them openly. Comment on the nature of such terms, and on the frequency of their use.

2. Using the Ngram viewer,[1] check (and comment on) the frequency with which the expressions *Damn it all!* and *God damn!* have been used over time.

3. Using the Ngram viewer, check (and comment on) the frequency with which the expression *radical Islam* was used from 1960 through 2008.

4. Using the Ngram viewer, check (and comment on) the frequency with which the expression *Christian*

---

1   For a quick introduction to the Ngram viewer, see the section entitled "How to Use This Book" at the beginning of the volume.

extremist was used from 1920 through 2008. What evidence can you find as to the frequency with which this term has been used since then?

5. Add the phrase *Islamic extremist* to the above search on your Ngram viewer, and comment on the use of the two terms (*Christian extremist* and *Islamic extremist*) through 2008.

6. Research the range of meanings of *jihad*. Then, using the Ngram viewer, check the frequency with which the word *jihad* has been used over time. What meanings of *jihad* do you think account for the increase in the word's usage? Should the word be used as frequently as it is?

7. Add the word *Crusade* on your Ngram viewer, and comment on the use of the two terms (*jihad* and *Crusade*) through 2008.

8. Using the Ngram viewer, check (and comment on) the frequency with which the expressions *Merry Christmas* and *Happy Hanukkah* have been used over time.

9. Explore the meanings of the derogatory term *papist*, and, using the Ngram viewer, check (and comment on) the frequency with which the word was used from 1700 through 2008.

religion

SEXUAL ORIENTATION

There remains a great deal of confusion in North America over what constitutes acceptable language regarding sexual orientation. We can start with those very words—*sexual orientation*. That term has for the most part now replaced *sexual preference* when it comes to describing gay, lesbian, bisexual, heterosexual, and other sexualities—and for a good reason. The word "preference" carries with it a connotation of choice—the notion that one *chooses* whether or not to be gay. It was on that sort of presumption that past generations tried to "cure" people of same sex desires. It's on that presumption too that some still refer to a "gay lifestyle," as if sexual orientation were akin to deciding either to settle down in a quiet, leafy suburb or travel around the world as a backpacker. In fact, of course, gay, lesbian, and bisexual people choose from among just as many lifestyles as do heterosexual people. And, as a great many scientific studies have shown, most gays and lesbians no more "choose" to be attracted to members of the same sex than most heterosexuals "choose" to be attracted to members of the opposite sex. Nor do bisexuals typically choose to be bisexual; they simply find themselves attracted to individuals of more than one sex.

When describing other people's relationships, it is also important to avoid redundant references to sexual orientation. In some contexts, unduly emphasizing sexual orientation can imply that LGBTQ people and their relationships are completely different from or are inferior to straight people and theirs:

needs checking   Dennis and Christopher have been a gay couple for years, but only recently had a same-sex wedding.

> *revised* Dennis and Christopher have been a couple for years, but only recently got married.

This is not to suggest that the word *gay* should be swept under the rug, just that it should not be overused in situations where sexual orientation is irrelevant or is already obvious from the names or pronouns being used. It would, for instance, be perfectly appropriate to refer to the opinions of *one gay couple in Mississippi, who asked to remain anonymous* in a discussion of equal marriage rights.

gay/homosexual

The term *gay* is now preferred to the term *homosexual*; why is that? Because of its history, is the short answer. The term *homosexual* was for so many generations used as a term of abuse—and, in the medical profession, as a term naming a form of mental illness—that it has now become tainted. Consequently, it is inappropriate to use phrases such as *homosexual sex* or *homosexual relationship* in most contexts; these phrases in particular are frequently used in anti-gay rhetoric to evoke the connotations of deviance and mental illness that *homosexual* can carry. That said, there are still a variety of contexts in which the word *homosexual* may (and should) still be used. One such context is the discussion of other historical eras in which a term such as "gay" would be anachronistic and "homosexual" may better reflect the terminology and cultural categories of the time. If a historian, for example, wants to speak of "the cultural construction of homosexual love in the nineteenth century," it would be misleading to replace "homosexual" with "gay."

sexual orientation

"That's so gay"

Soon after the word *gay* came to be recommended in the late twentieth century as the preferred non-pejorative term for same-sex sexual orientation, the expression "that's so gay" began to be widely used in conversation by young people. Its meaning? "That's really stupid," or "That's weak and ineffectual." But inevitably such usages connect at some level with other meanings; it's impossible if you use such a term to avoid a broader association of what is gay with what is stupid, weak, and ineffectual. (Imagine if people started to use the expression "that's so white" or "that's so Black" or "that's so Christian" to mean "that's really stupid.") Much as many have protested that "that's so gay" is an "innocent expression," it's not. The cumulative repetition of this and similar colloquial expressions does a great deal to reinforce human prejudice against gays, lesbians, and bisexuals, and to make it more difficult for those who are gay to be open about it, and proud of it.

queer

What of the term *queer*? For much of the twentieth century *queer* and *faggot* were the most common terms of abuse hurled at gays and lesbians. In the last quarter of the last century, however, many gays began to defiantly claim the term as their own—in the process declaring their difference from what was felt (with good reason) to be the straightjacket of straight society. "We're queer and we're here—get used to it"[1] became a familiar chant at gay rallies and protests.

---

1 A variant has long been used in cities such as Vancouver during the annual Pride parade as marchers move through the downtown retail district, or demonstrate at malls: "We're here; we're queer; we're not going shopping!"

As with other terms of abuse that have been reclaimed by members of the group that has been on the receiving end of the abuse, use of the term *queer* should not be taken lightly by those who are not members of the victimized group. But while with cases such as *nigga* the right approach is straightforward—those not part of the group the word is used to disparage should simply never use the word—the case of *queer* is more complicated. While many gay, lesbian, bisexual, and transgender people feel that the word is inherently and extremely offensive, the word has also been taken up by others in ways that call upon people outside the community to use it. In the humanities, *queer theory* (a branch of critical theory) attaches specific meanings to the word *queer*, and the word can and should be used as an academic term in that context. Many activists also use phrases such as *queer community* to refer to all people whose sexual orientation or gender identity challenges cultural norms; the commonly used alternative, *LGBT* (an acronym meaning *lesbian/gay/bisexual/transgender*),[1] is seen by some as less inclusive because it does not—and could not possibly—name all of the incredibly diverse identity markers that fall under the umbrella of *queer*. (Many now extend *LGBT* to *LGBTQ*—see below.) And some people with whom the radical tone or the open-ended meaning of *queer* resonates prefer to identify themselves as *queer* in addition to—or even instead of—*gay*, *lesbian*, or anything else. The bottom line is that some audiences will find the use of *queer* alienating and offensive while others will find it inclusive and celebratory, so it is

sexual orientation

1   Sometimes a *Q* for *queer* and/or *questioning* is added to the end of the acronym; some organizations use longer acronyms to acknowledge other identity markers, such as *asexual*, *intersex*, and *pansexual*; the shorter acronym *LGB* is used to refer exclusively to sexual orientation as distinct from gender identity.

important to take care when deciding whether or not to use the word in a given context.

bisexual invisibility

In the United States, more people identify as bisexual than as gay or lesbian combined,[1] but bisexuals and bisexual issues are too frequently ignored both in heterosexual and in gay and lesbian communities. The problem of bisexual invisibility manifests itself in all sorts of ways. Bisexuality is often treated as though it is merely a phase rather than a legitimate sexual orientation (even though research shows this is not the case), and community programs and organizations that are ostensibly for all LGBTQ people often leave out bisexuals in practice.

To avoid making bisexuality invisible in your language, avoid using the phrase *gay and lesbian* on its own if what you are saying also applies to bisexual people (see the discussion of *queer* above for some alternative terms). But avoiding bisexual invisibility is more than a matter of terminology; it is important not to assume or imply through your language that everyone in a same-sex relationship is always gay— or that everyone in an opposite-sex relationship is always heterosexual.

Unpacking LGBTQ*: A Sampling of Identity Terms

Many people whose identities fall under the LGBTQ* umbrella identify their gender or sexual orientation as something other than, or in addition to, *lesbian*, *gay*, *bisexual*,

---

1   See the San Francisco Human Rights Commission's report "Bisexual Invisibility: Impacts and Recommendations" (2011) for these and other statistics.

transgender, or *queer*—a fact that is often indicated with an asterisk or plus sign placed at the end of the acronym. There is an incredibly diverse range of terms used by LGBTQ* people to describe identities, and this range of possible identifications continues to grow and evolve as the community does. Only a few of these are touched on below; it would be impossible even to list all of the relevant terms here.

Note that the way these terms are used varies by region and from person to person. It is thus impossible to know what it means to a given individual to be *asexual,* or *genderqueer,* or *third gender* without asking them. The best thing, if you need to describe or understand other people's sexual orientations or gender identities and you are in a context where it is appropriate to do so, is to ask them how they interpret the terms they use to identify themselves.

agender

People may identify as agender if they identify as having no gender at all, as having a neutral gender that is neither male nor female, or as not having or not wanting a term to describe their gender.

androsexual

An androsexual person is sexually attracted to men and/or masculine gender expressions. This term—with its complement, *gynesexual*—is often taken up by people with nonbinary genders because it describes only the gender one finds attractive.

asexual

An asexual person is one who rarely or never experiences sexual attraction to other people, and/or rarely or never desires sex with other people. Note that *asexuality* is an orientation, while *celibacy* is a practice, and the two words are not synonyms: asexual people sometimes have sex, and many celibate people are not asexual. Asexual communities often recognize romantic as distinct from sexual attraction; both sexual and asexual people may identify as *aromantic*, *heteroromantic*, *biromantic*, *homoromantic*, and so on. *Ace* is a common short form for *asexual*, similar in function to *gay* or *bi*.

gender fluid or genderfluid

A genderfluid person is a combination of male, female, and/or other genders; which gender the person identifies with most strongly changes over time.

genderqueer

The term *genderqueer* includes people who identify as having no gender, as both male and female, as gender fluid, or as anything else other than strictly "male" or "female." Some people use *genderqueer* as the only term to describe their gender identities; for others, it is an umbrella term that encompasses a range of more specific identities. According to some definitions, *genderqueer* also applies to people who "queer" gender—who express gender in a way that contradicts or draws attention to gender norms—even if such individuals do identify as exclusively male or female.

sexual orientation

pansexual

A pansexual person is one who can experience sexual attraction to people of all genders. According to some definitions, the term *pansexual* also applies to people who can be attracted to others of many genders, but not all; by other definitions, the term *polysexual* applies instead in these cases. Whether *bisexual* and *pansexual* are synonyms is a matter of debate.

skoliosexual

A person may identify as skoliosexual if they are specifically attracted to genderqueer, transgender, and or transsexual people. This term, which emerged in the early 2010s, is controversial. Some argue that it legitimizes the fetishization of trans people and undermines the legitimacy of trans gender identities. Others, however, argue that the term accurately describes a real orientation and that skoliosexuality no more requires the fetishization of trans people than being a lesbian necessarily involves the fetishization of women.

third gender

A third-gender person does not identify as either a man or a woman, but as both, neither, or something else. Though individuals who identify with this term interpret it in various ways, it is also used in reference to third options for gender identification on government documents and in reference to specific groups in societies that recognize more than two sexes. In India and some other countries in South Asia, for example, *hijras* are identified as third-gender in government documentation.

sexual orientation

two-spirit

Any Aboriginal North American who is not cisgendered and/or is not heterosexual might identify as two-spirit. The term reflects differences between traditional Aboriginal gender roles and those imposed by colonization; many North American tribes traditionally have conceptualized at least one gender role that incorporates aspects of both male and female roles; such gender roles often entail specific artistic or spiritual responsibilities. The term *two-spirit*, which refers to the idea common across many tribes that an individual can possess both male and female spirits, is a pan-Indian term used all over North America for a range of identities that extend beyond traditional two-spirit roles. There are also, however, many terms that belong to individual tribes (e.g., *lhaman*, used by the Zuni; *lila witkowin* and *winkte*, used by the Lakota; and *a'yahkwêw*, used by the Plains Cree); these may be more appropriate in some contexts.

Many fuller lists of LGBTQ* terminology are available online; one particularly useful resource is the "Comprehensive* List of LGBTQ+ Term Definitions" found on itspronouncedmetrosexual.com.

sexual orientation

A CASE TO CONSIDER

Heteronormative Assumptions

Here is the gist of a true-life exchange that occurred recently in a class at a small west coast university. The topic of discussion was the language of love; the third stanza of W.H. Auden's poem "Funeral Blues" was raised as an example of extravagant thoughts expressed in plain language:

> He was my North, my South, my East and West,
> My working week and my Sunday rest,
> My noon, my midnight, my talk, my song;
> I thought that love would last for ever: I was
> wrong.

One student made the following comment about what the speaker says here: "When poets write love poems, most of the time they leave work out of the picture; they make it seem as if love is something that happens outside of the working day. This poet, on the other hand, says that her lover was her 'working week' as well as her 'Sunday rest.' And of course she's right that when you're in a loving relationship it affects your whole life—including when you're at work."

The instructor praised the student but also gently corrected her on one point: "I think that's a very good observation about love and work. I had better also mention, though, that W.H. Auden was a *he*, not a *she*."

The student: "But that can't be right: the poet refers to the dead lover as *he*; she can't be a *he* herself!"

At which point another student (known by many others in the class to be gay) began to laugh, and the laughter gradually spread round the class until finally the first speaker got it and began to laugh too—as well as to apologize.

Questions and Suggestions for Discussion

1. Explore the etymology of the expression *Boston marriage*.

2. Using the *Oxford English Dictionary*, explore the meanings of the term *homosocial*; and, using the Ngram viewer,[1] check the frequency with which that word has been used over time. How might we explain the rapid increase in frequency of use in the 1980s and 1990s, and the decline after 2000?

3. Using the Ngram viewer, check (and comment on) the frequency with which the following expressions have been used over time: *he's gay*; *he's homosexual*; *he's a homosexual*; *he's queer*.

4. Using the Ngram viewer, compare (and comment on) the frequency with which the following derogatory expressions have been used between 1850 and 2008: *he's a fairy*; *he's a faggot*; *she's a dyke*.

5. Explore the etymology of the words *buggery* and *bugger* (the latter both as a noun and as a verb). As well, using the Ngram viewer, check (and comment on) the historical patterns as to frequency of use of these terms from 1750 through to 2008. Why might use of the term *buggery* have increased so steeply in the late eighteenth and again in the late twentieth centuries?

---

1 For a quick introduction to the Ngram viewer, see the section entitled "How to Use This Book" at the beginning of the volume.

POLITICAL CONTROVERSIES

illegal immigration

It's hard to answer the question of what might be wrong with the phrase *illegal immigrant* without addressing the rights and wrongs of the immigration system itself. In the United States these issues have become particularly contested. The system itself, many argue, is founded on hypocrisy. Companies in various sectors of the economy (notably agriculture) have developed a cost/price model based on workers receiving far less than what most Americans consider to be a living wage. Governments have assisted them in setting up this model through legislation creating lower minimum wage rates for categories such as agricultural workers—and by turning a blind eye when businesses illegally hire undocumented workers to fill those jobs at rates of pay that no American citizen would be willing to accept. Wealthy individuals often hire workers on a similar basis to care for their gardens or for their children. Average citizens may regard themselves as blameless in all this—but the average citizen continues to expect that food will be priced at levels that would be impossible to achieve if all workers were making a decent wage. (In inflation-adjusted dollars, the cost of food to North Americans has declined fairly steadily for many decades; whereas in 1950 food made up about one-third of the typical family's total expenditures, in 2013 it made up just 14%.)[1] Few demand higher food prices and better wages

---

1   See Stephen B. Reed, "One Hundred Years of Price Change: The Consumer Price Index and the American Inflation Experience," *Monthly Labor Review*, April 2014. In Canada (where a good deal of food is imported from the U.S., and where much agricultural labor is also carried out by migrant (cont'd)

for workers; many cry out for a crackdown on the illegal immigration on which the cheap food/cheap landscaping/cheap child care system that they benefit from depends.[1]

What does all this have to do with the term *illegal immigrant*? Arguably, this term unduly stigmatizes people for working and living in a way that is ostensibly against the law but which the North American economy depends on.[2] Why call the immigrants illegal, but not, for example, the businesses and individuals who employ them illegally?

Even if one does not take this view, terms such as *illegal immigrant*, *illegal alien*, and *illegal* (used by itself as a noun) should nonetheless be avoided, simply because they are factually inaccurate: they imply that the people themselves—rather than the actions they or their parents may have taken—are illegal. (*Alien* on its own should also be avoided where possible[3] for its obviously dehumanizing association with beings from outer space.) One better option is to use

---

workers, who are often paid low, piece-work rates rather than an hourly rate), food represented about 30% of the spending of the average household in the first half of the twentieth century; it now represents 16%. See "Exploring the First Century of Canada's Consumer Price Index," *Statistics Canada*, 2015.

1   This is of course not the only cause. It has also depended on increases in productivity brought about by agricultural research—and on the spread of the factory farming of non-human animals.

2   Canadians tend to think of this issue as being relevant only to the United States—but of course a very high percentage of the produce that Canadians consume is imported from the United States and is low-priced in large part because American agricultural workers (many of them undocumented) are so poorly paid. Within Canada most agricultural workers are documented, but that does not mean they are treated fairly; under the little-known Seasonal Agricultural Worker Program roughly 30,000 workers come to Canada for several months each year. Legally, these workers are "exempt from labor laws that govern minimum wage, overtime, and rest periods." (See Denise Balkissoon, "Migrant Farm Workers Deserve Better from Canada," *The Globe and Mail*, 19 September 2016.)

3   "Illegal alien" and "alien" are legal terms in America and several other countries, so it may not always be practical to completely avoid using them.

phrases such as *people who have immigrated illegally*—which has the added advantage of emphasizing that the immigrants being discussed are people—but where that approach is too wordy, there are a range of acceptable alternatives. Popular choices include *undocumented immigrants* or *undocumented workers*, though critics of these terms argue that many such immigrants *do* in fact have documentation—just not the correct documentation. A less common but less controversial choice is *unauthorized immigrants*.[1]

mass killings

In 1995, a 26-year-old American Gulf War veteran who had been influenced by the Christian Identity movement killed 168 innocent people in Oklahoma City. In 2011 a 32-year-old Norwegian man who described himself as "100 percent Christian" killed 77 innocent people (many of them children). Should these people be called Christian extremists, or right-wing extremists, or terrorists, or simply shooters and bombers? In 1994 a 37-year-old Israeli doctor who professed his faith in Judaism killed 29 innocent people at prayer; should he be called a Jewish extremist, or a Zionist extremist, or a terrorist, or simply a shooter? Various people professing faith in Hinduism killed over 1,000 innocent Muslims in the Indian state of Gujarat in 2002; should they be called Hindu radicals, or Hindu extremists, or terrorists, or simply mass killers?

Because most of the terms we use to refer to people who commit bombings, mass shootings, and similar crimes imply something about the motive behind the killing, it is

---

1   It is also worth noting that in the U.K. the word *immigrant* has taken on derogatory connotations to the extent that many conscientious British writers now use *migrant* instead.

often difficult to decide what term to use in any particular case. Be cognizant of a common pattern in North American media in which a person of color who commits a mass killing is more readily described as a *terrorist* or as a religious or political *extremist*, while a white person who commits the same sort of crime is more likely to be described as a *lone wolf*, *lone gunman*, or *loner*. All three of the latter terms were used, for example, by major newspapers[1] to describe the young white man who killed nine people at the Emanuel African Methodist Episcopal Church in Charleston, South Carolina in 2015—whose crime was clearly motivated by a political belief in white supremacy. The effect of this double standard is not only that it leads us to overlook important patterns in white culture (dismissing this killer as a "loner" excuses us from considering the culture of racism that motivated his crime). The double standard also encourages another unfortunate tendency: when a person of color commits a mass killing that is identified as an "act of terrorism," others of the same race are in too many minds also branded as potential terrorists. In an editorial for Al Jazeera, Elmaz Abinader describes the experiences of Arab- and Muslim-Americans waiting, in the aftermath of a mass killing, for the identity of the killer to be revealed:

> … [W]e waited. Not Arabs, not Muslims, not "terrorists," we hoped.

---

1   For example, *lone wolf* appears in *USA Today* ("'Lone Wolf' Attacks Are Difficult to Detect—And Difficult to Prevent," 22 June 2015); *lone gunman* appears in *The New York Times* (Chris Dixon, "Prosecutors to Seek Death Penalty … in Charleston Shootings," 3 September 2015); and *loner* appears in *The Wall Street Journal* (Jennifer Levitz and John Kamp, "Charleston Shooting Suspect … Became a Loner in Recent Years," 18 June 2015). Though *USA Today* quotes a "terrorism analyst" in its article, none of the quoted articles use the word *terrorist*.

> Because we—Arab Americans, Muslim Americans—know that while "mass shootings" conducted by white men are assigned to an individual, acts of "terrorism" belong to an entire community....
>
> So we waited—knowing what the consequences would be if the shooters this time were not only "shooters" but "terrorists." The vitriolic condemnation of religion, race and cultural background would be inflamed and would wreak havoc on our individual and collective psyches....
>
> ... We will not be allowed to dissociate ourselves from them as everyone else can from those white, male "mass shooters" who represent no one but themselves.[1]

Note also that, when discussing mass killings, many conscientious writers avoid using the names of the perpetrators so as to avoid giving them undeserved fame; for a discussion of this practice, see the "Cases to Consider" at the end of this section.

prostitution/sex work/commercial sex

When it comes to the controversial issue of exchanging money for sex, one of the most fraught language issues is what to call people who engage in this practice. It should be obvious that—unless one works in the sex trade oneself—one should avoid using words such as *whore* and *hooker*, or any of the dozens of other overtly derogatory words English offers for this purpose. (Unconscionably,

---

1   See "When Is a Mass Shooting More than a Mass Shooting?," 4 December 2015.

many people continue to use the word *whore* as a pejorative term intended to demean not just women who work in the sex trade, but any woman who has been or is thought to have been sexually active; it is still all too common for a man who sleeps with a series of partners to be referred to admiringly as a *stud* or a *player*, while a woman who behaves in the same way is referred to contemptuously as a *whore* or a *slut*.[1] There are few more distasteful aspects of North American society than this.)

It is one thing to be clear about the word *whore*. But what of the word *prostitute*? Activists generally agree that this word, too, ought to be avoided because it carries with it an enormous amount of prejudice regarding the gender, morality, and human value of the people it labels. Many activists suggest instead the phrase *sex worker*—a phrase that is gender neutral and relatively free of cultural baggage, and that treats sex work as a job much like any other. (In this, *sex work* contrasts with *sex trafficking*, in which the participants are coerced; many activists argue that forced participation in the sex trade must be distinguished from sex work as a chosen job.) The economic terminology of *sex work* is extended to people who hire sex workers—traditionally called *johns*, but now often referred to as *clients* or *customers*. (It is worth noting that *sex worker* can have a broader meaning than *prostitute*, applying to anyone who works in the sex industry—including porn actors, strippers, and so on.)

Though *sex worker* is the most commonly preferred term, it is important to acknowledge that it is not accepted by all activists. In particular, those who believe that the sale of sex for money can never be a healthy or freely chosen

---

1   See also the separate discussion of *slut* in these pages.

career argue that *sex worker* should not be used because it suggests that "sex work" should be thought of as a job, as opposed to a form of abuse. (This is, of course, the reason why many other activists embrace the term so readily.) In contrast, those who wish to emphasize the damaging aspects of commercial sex use terms such as *prostituted women* or *men*, or *victims* or *survivors of commercial sexual exploitation*. Terms such as *client* or *customer* are, similarly, replaced by *offender* or *exploiter*. Unsurprisingly, the terms writers use tend to reflect their opinions regarding how commercial sex should be treated under the law; users of *sex worker* tend to support legalization, while users of *commercial sexual exploitation* tend to argue that paying for sex should be a criminal offense.

Regardless of what terminology you choose, be careful not to use language that unduly highlights someone's involvement in the sex trade:

worth checking   In a well-known case, a Port Coquitlam man killed dozens of sex workers before police began a serious investigation.

[It may be that this sentence is part of a passage addressing the fact that the women who were killed were from a vulnerable population; in other contexts, however, mentioning that the victims were in the sex trade might serve to distance them from supposedly "normal" or "good" women—thereby downplaying the seriousness of the violence.]

revised   In a well-known case, a Port Coquitlam man killed dozens of women before police began a serious investigation.

Even when not talking about commercial sex directly, it's worth making an effort to think through the implications of expressions that reference the sex trade. Quite clearly, to refer to someone as a *whore* is to give expression to a repugnant double standard regarding sexuality itself. But even a joke expression such as *I'd whore myself out for a decent cheeseburger* is problematic. So too is using *prostitution* as a metaphor for selling out or doing something inherently degrading (*I won't prostitute myself for that gossip column anymore; I'm going to focus on finishing my novel*).

CASES TO CONSIDER

Opposing Views on Abortion and Language

Don's View:

Which term does a better job of representing the views of its adherents—*pro-life* or *pro-choice*?

Arguably, neither.

Who is against the idea of choice? Who is against life itself? No one, surely. Yet the terms *pro-choice* and *pro-life* continue to be commonly used by, respectively, those who support the idea that a pregnant person has the right to have an abortion and those who oppose the idea that people have any such right. In both cases, the words seem designed to slant the terms of the debate by implying that the opposing side is against choice of any kind, in the one case, or against life itself, in the other.

The problem with terms that "load the dice" in this sort of way may be more clear if we think of analogous situations.

Imagine if the opponents of genetically modified food styled themselves as *the pro-nature movement*—or that its supporters styled themselves as *the pro-families movement* (on the grounds that families benefit from the low prices that genetically modified food makes possible). Imagine if the supporters of the practice of fracking styled themselves as *the pro-prosperity movement* and the opponents styled themselves as *the pro-earth movement*. Virtually no one is against the earth, or families, or nature, or prosperity; each of these terms thus carries with it an unfortunate implication about those on the other side of the debate.

So how should we speak of abortion? There's a good argument to be made for speaking of it as just that—*abortion*. In the same way that it makes sense to speak of fracking as *fracking* and genetically modified food as *genetically modified food*, it makes sense to speak of abortion as *abortion*.

There's a further argument here as well. The more we shy away from the word *abortion*, the more we stigmatize abortion itself—a procedure which, to my mind, should not in any way be regarded as intrinsically wrong. Too often, it seems to me, it is assumed that abortion should always be regarded as inherently regrettable; it is a medical procedure that, more than any other, comes with a stigma, sometimes even from those who support a woman's right to choose that procedure. And I simply don't believe it should have that stigma attached to it. On its own, the human body terminates pregnancies all the time; by some counts, two out of every three fertilized eggs are aborted spontaneously. If, to take a specific example, a woman chooses to end her pregnancy early, after testing has revealed that the foetus is malformed or will suffer from a serious disability if the woman does give birth, she is doing very much the same sort of thing that the human body does very frequently of its own accord. Is it obvious that abortion is a regrettable choice—that it would be a good thing to carry a foetus to term and to give birth in such circumstances? The *circumstances* may be regrettable—but the same surely should not be said for making the option of a safe, medical abortion available. To my mind it should go without saying that whether or not to give birth or have an abortion should be the woman's choice—but I also think that all of us should resist any impulse to regard abortion as a choice that is always or inherently regrettable.

Every case is different, of course, and I certainly would not want to suggest that abortion is never regrettable. To take a very different example, it seems to me to be regrettable that some women—perhaps I should say some families, for in such cases the woman is often prevented from making a truly autonomous choice—choose abortion as a way of making sure they have a male child and not a female one. But again, my disagreement would be with the choice made in that particular case—not with the right of the person to choose, and not with abortion itself, which I would argue should not in any way be stigmatized. If we stigmatize the word, we stigmatize the procedure—and it absolutely should not be stigmatized.

If we do speak of abortion as *abortion*, it seems relatively unproblematic to describe someone who opposes the legality of abortion as *anti-abortion*. But what about someone who argues that abortions should be legal? *Pro-abortion* does not quite work, since it could easily be taken to imply that a "pro-abortion" person wants as many abortions to be performed as possible—an implication that is hardly fair, since most supporters of legal abortion are not advocating the extinction of the human race, or suggesting that abortion should be the only option for people facing unwanted pregnancies. One widely used alternative is *pro-abortion rights*, which much more accurately reflects the nature of the argument.

It's not just a matter of accuracy, though. One effect of using terms such as *pro-life* and *pro-choice* may be to further politicize a topic that many feel is excessively politicized already. Would a change in the language that is used to frame the issue in countries such as the United States perhaps contribute to a change in attitudes as well? If we avoid terms such as *pro-life* and *pro-choice*, might it become easier to discuss abortion not as a political issue but as a medical issue (albeit a medical issue with ethical implications, as is the case with so many medical issues)?[1] If so, that would to my mind be a very good thing.

Laura's View:

If asked, I describe myself as *pro-choice*. The term *pro-abortion rights* also describes me, but it is not the term I use. I use *pro-choice* because, to me, the term emphasizes two key parts of the debate: the importance of actual access to abortion and the importance of bodily autonomy.

My belief is that all pregnant people should be able to decide whether or not to carry their pregnancies to term, and that therefore the option of an abortion should be available to everyone. This means more than just that

---

1   It's often assumed that, one way or another, any country has to have some law governing abortion on the books. But that's not in fact the case. In Canada, for example, there has been no such law since 1988, when the Canadian Supreme Court ruled the previous law unconstitutional.

political controversies

abortion ought to be legal—a position that might seem to be suggested by *abortion rights*. In order for abortion to be a legitimate choice for everyone who might want to choose it, it must be accessible to people in rural areas as well as in big cities, and in every region; it must be free to anyone who could not otherwise afford it; and every health care worker with patients considering abortion must inform them about their options without bullying them into any particular decision.

Don suggests that no-one is "against choice," and that the term *pro-choice* slants the terms of the debate by implying that the opposing side is against choice of any kind. But in this context, *pro-choice* does not seem to me to describe choice of every kind; it is used to describe choice regarding one's own body. I would argue that those who believe abortion should be illegal under all or most circumstances *are* accurately described as anti-choice; their position is that pregnant people should not have a choice about whether or not to remain pregnant. Given that in many parts of North America the campaign to restrict the bodily autonomy of pregnant people is succeeding—I appreciate *pro-choice* as a reminder that we are considering the question of whether or not pregnant people are able to choose what happens to their own bodies.

Don offers some examples of situations in which individuals might choose abortion, and points out that, regardless of his personal agreement with any particular decision an individual might make, he supports a pregnant person's right to choose whether or not to abort. I would take an even stronger stance than this: imagining the circumstances under which someone might choose abortion is a useful exercise in empathy, but when it comes to abortion I also question whether it is a good idea to foreground talk of which choices we may or may not approve. Any discussion of this sort should not be allowed to cloud what is to me the central issue: whether people—including pregnant people—should be enabled to choose what happens to their own bodies. I consider no choice a pregnant person makes with regard to abortion to be regrettable, so long as that choice is made freely. I support fully the choices of pregnant people who have abortions because the foetus is unlikely to develop into a healthy child; or because they live in a society where women are severely oppressed and do not want to birth a girl into a life of suffering; or because they already have the number of children they feel they can take care of; or because they do not want children yet, or perhaps ever; or because they simply do not want to undergo pregnancy; or for any number of other reasons. (And, I would add, I support equally pregnant people's choices to have a baby with a severe disability, or to have a family despite economic hardship, or to carry a pregnancy to term and then choose adoption—and so on.) The key point is that every pregnant person, regardless of circumstances, should have a choice—and the term *pro-choice* emphasizes precisely that.

What about *pro-abortion*? Sure, I am *pro-abortion* for people who want or need this procedure, in the sense that I am pro-modern medicine in general—including, for example, for people who want or need procedures such as in vitro fertilization in order to become pregnant. But just as I would like fewer people to have unwanted medical issues of all sorts, I would like fewer people to find themselves in a position to want or need abortions. And I would like to accomplish this by offering more choices to people who are or might become pregnant: better access to methods of birth control; better child-care options, especially for parents with lower incomes; changes in public policy to reduce the frequency of rape; and so on. For me, then, *pro-choice* understood broadly is not just about abortion but about all kinds of choice surrounding reproductive rights.[1]

Fat and Language

It might seem self-evident that a thoughtful English speaker should never use the word *fat* to describe another person—the word is, to many, inherently insulting. But many activists advocating for the better treatment of fat people disagree: using euphemisms to skirt the issue of fat, such activists argue, implies that fatness is something other than a neutral fact about a person's body. As the writer Sarai Walker argues in her opinion piece "Yes, I'm Fat. It's O.K. I Said It,"

> fat activists use the word proudly in an effort to destigmatize not only the word, but by exten-sion, the fat body…. [F]at—not just the word, but fatness itself—is apparently so horrible it's unspeakable.[2]

---

1   I should acknowledge here that my interpretation of *pro-choice* differs from that of many women of color who associate the pro-choice movement with the narrowly focused goal of making and keeping abortion legal. As the critic Verónica Bayetti Flores claims, "women of color have long known that the idea of 'choice' is a privileged position, that it has never felt familiar to many of us, and that our liberation required a lot more than lofty Supreme Court decisions that gave us the theoretical choice to terminate our pregnancies." Many activists who hold such views suggest replacing the framework of *choice* with one of *reproductive justice*, a term that groups abortion with other issues related to reproduction, from forced sterilization to economic inequal-ity (since many pregnant people who are financially unable to provide for children find themselves essentially forced into abortions by poverty). (See Verónica Bayetti Flores, "#Knowyourhistory: Women of Color Have Been Moving beyond 'Pro-Choice' for Decades," *Feministing* 2014.)

2   *The New York Times*, 6 February 2016.

As Marilyn Wann advocates in her preface to *The Fat Studies Reader* (2009, NYU Press), fat activists use *fat* "both as the preferred neutral adjective (i.e., short/tall, young/old, fat/thin) and also as a preferred term of political identity" because "[t]here is nothing negative or rude in the word *fat* unless someone makes the effort to put it there."

In some areas of formal writing, the terms *overweight* and *obese* are considered the preferred alternatives to *fat*, but fat activists have also raised objections to these. Wann points out that

> "Overweight" is inherently anti-fat. It implies an extreme goal: instead of a bell curve distribution of human weights, it calls for a lone, towering, unlikely bar graph with everyone occupying the same (thin) weights.

The word *obese* Wann condemns as "medicaliz[ing]." In other words, it captures an attitude toward fatness that classifies it as a public health issue—and therefore justifies public judgment of fat individuals—while also denying fat people the compassion normally offered to sick people because "no one really believes that being fat is any kind of disease."

But what about the argument that fatness really is a serious medical concern, and that we should therefore avoid giving the impression in our language that fatness is acceptable? This is a common position; as Carol Weston put it in a letter to *The New York Times*, "Obesity is a public health problem, and healthy self-esteem should not come at the price of health."[1] Against this, some fat activists, such as those associated with the Health at Every Size movement,

---

1   See "How We View Obesity," 13 February 2016.

would argue that it is in fact possible to eat well, exercise regularly, and maintain an otherwise healthy lifestyle while carrying a high percentage of body fat—and also point out that many people who do not take good care of their bodies are nonetheless thin. Why not place the primary emphasis on healthy behaviors rather than on size?

Even if we take for granted that a weight outside of a certain range tends to carry health risks, it is still a big leap to argue that this justifies shaming fat people to the extent that North Americans typically do. As Wann argues, "It is not possible to hate a group of people for [the group's] own good."[1] And even if shaming could somehow lead to positive health consequences, Walker points out, it is unacceptable that "the dignity of any group should be contingent on whether its members are deemed healthy." That concern about health often serves as a cover for disparaging the humanity of fat people is suggested by the difference that emerges when we speak about most other ways that people endanger their health. We don't euphemistically

---

1 It would be difficult to argue against the claim that discrimination has a negative impact on fat people. Apart from its impact on self-esteem—which is important in itself—fatphobia has significant material effects. Numerous studies have shown that obese job applicants are less likely to be hired than other applicants, regardless of qualifications or personality, and that fat employees—especially women—tend to make less money. One 1990 study found that "among those 50% or more above their ideal weight ... 17% reported being fired or pressured to resign because of their weight." Fat students are significantly less likely to be accepted to university or college, despite there being no difference between fat and thin students' average academic performance. Fat discrimination even, ironically, has an impact on health: fat people—again, especially women—are more likely to avoid or put off going to the doctor, especially for preventative treatment such as gynecological exams. This reluctance to obtain medical care is unsurprising, given the attitudes common among medical professionals; 39% of doctors in one survey described their obese patients as "lazy," while 24% of nurses, when surveyed, said that caring for obese patients "repulsed them." (For these and other statistics on fat discrimination, see Rebecca Puhl and Kelly D. Brownell, "Bias, Discrimination, and Obesity," *Obesity: A Research Journal*, vol. 9, no. 12, 2012.)

describe smokers as "tobacco-inclined,"[1] and we don't normally use medical terminology when we want to say that someone works a high-stress job.

This does not, however, mean that using the word *fat* is a good idea in every circumstance. If your friend asks *How do I look in this outfit?*, you might want to consider the reception you'll get if you answer *Fat and fabulous!* Because *fat* has long been—and still is—used as a dehumanizing slur, it is possible that the use of *fat* with positive intention will still come across as an insult. *Fat* is also a vague term—how much body fat does a person have to have in order to qualify as fat?—so using it can put a writer in the position of describing other people as fat who would not describe themselves that way.

Despite the reasonable objections of some fat activists, some writers find that words or phrases such as *plus size, heavy, larger,* or *people with a high BMI* can provide the best solution in situations where the positive use of *fat* might not come across to most readers. And it may be very difficult to avoid using *obese* and *overweight* rather than *fat* in some contexts; these remain the standard words in journalism, and they are used in scientific writing to refer to specific BMI (Body Mass Index) measurements. (Some fat activists work around this by placing *obese* and *overweight* in quotation marks so as to use the words without endorsing them.)

Whether or not one embraces the use of the word *fat*, it is important not to use it or any other term unthinkingly, but

---

1 This is not to suggest that smokers never face discrimination—on the contrary, especially in hiring situations, discrimination against smokers is a real problem—but that smoking addiction is not considered as "unspeakable" as fatness because western culture does not dehumanize smokers in the same way.

to remain sensitive to what language choices imply about fatness and fat people. But there are some basic rules that can be universally applied: obviously, avoid using *fat* as a slur (*he's nothing but a fat slob*; *she's a fat pig*) and avoid using other slurs that disparage fat people. Similarly, avoid using *fat* as though it had an inherently negative meaning (*Ick, I feel so fat after all that pizza*; *Do I look fat in this shirt?*). Also avoid references to "normal" weight—a meaningless term (since not everyone has the same healthy weight) that is also misleading, since more than 69% of American and 61% of Canadian adults are categorized as "overweight" or "obese."[1] Finally, as with race, sexual orientation, and many other similar descriptors, when describing a fat individual it is always a good idea to consider whether that person's fatness is relevant to the context—and if it isn't, don't mention it.

Global Warming/Climate Change

At some point early in the second decade of this century many who were concerned about global warming started to feel that the phrase *global warming* was itself part of the problem. If it is vital to persuade human beings to take drastic action to keep our planet from being over-heated—specifically, to reduce the amount of CO_2 and other greenhouse gasses being released into the atmosphere—is it not also important to make the dangers of what might happen plain through the language we use? To most of us, *warming* is a word with pleasant associations; would it not be better to use a more neutral term? More than that, is it not appro-

political controversies

---

1   For these and other statistics, see the Harvard T.H. Chan School of Public Health Obesity Prevention Source Web Site and the Public Health Agency of Canada's report *Obesity in Canada* (2011).

priate to acknowledge that the effects of climate change will not be the same everywhere? Some areas will become unbearably hot; a few areas may even become permanently colder, even as the overall average temperature for the planet increases; other "changes," such as an increased frequency and intensity of hurricanes, are important concerns not captured by the phrase *global warming*. Nor will a warming pattern always occur in a straight line; within the broad pattern of climate change will be innumerable variations in any given area, such that for years at a time areas that are part of the warming pattern may temporarily become colder. Is it not better on those grounds too to use a term that is less likely to be taken to imply that the trend will be always and in all areas towards warmer temperatures?

So it was that *climate change* came to be the preferred term among many of those warning of the need for urgent action—and that use of the phrase *global warming* came to be frowned upon.

Not all have been persuaded, though. Even among those who are convinced both of the reality of the change and of the urgent need for action, a number feel that *global warming* in no way deserves banishment. After all, the phrase *climate change* could mean anything;[1] every coming of an ice age has been an instance of climate change. The phrase *global warming*, then, connects more directly with the sort of climate change that we are undergoing—the sort that

---

1   Witness Marco Rubio on the television program *Face the Nation* on 19 April 2015: "I believe the climate is changing because there's never been a moment where the climate is not changing. The question is, what percentage of [climate change today] ... is due to human activity? If we do the things they want us to do, cap-and-trade, you name it, how much will that change the pace of climate change versus how much will that cost to our economy? Scientists can't tell us what impact it would have on reversing these changes, but I can tell you, with certainty, it would have a devastating impact on our economy."

requires urgent action. Yes, different areas will be affected differently, but so far as the effect on the world as a whole is concerned, *global warming* is precisely the phenomenon that is the subject of discussion. And surely human beings are grown-up enough to understand that, much as the word *warming* may often carry with it positive associations, it need not always do so. To try to banish the expression *global warming* would be to treat them like children, just when we most want humans to think rationally and to act responsibly—for the sake of our children and our children's children as well as for ourselves.

What do you think? Should either term be considered acceptable? Do efforts to discredit the term *global warming* represent the sort of paternalism or "political correctness" that sometimes gives progressive causes a bad name? Or is it reasonable to name things with the hope of influencing people's actions? If so, will *climate change* achieve the desired results in this case? Which term more truly reflects the reality of what is going on? Is either term more likely than the other to breed misunderstanding?

Refugee Crisis, Migrant Crisis

In 2014, large numbers of people began to journey toward Europe seeking somewhere safer and better to live, leaving their homes in parts of the Middle East, Africa, and West Asia. The resulting crisis clearly merits discussion on a global scale, but should it be called a Migrant Crisis or a Refugee Crisis—and should the people who undertake such journeys be called migrants or refugees?

The question is highly charged politically, as both words carry implications regarding the motives of those who have left their home countries—and implications regarding the responsibilities other nations have to such individuals. *Refugees* are people who have fled their country to escape war or other threats to safety such as persecution or a natural disaster. The meaning of *migrants* is more controversial. Some claim that *migrant* is a neutral term describing any people who relocate across national borders for any reason, while others claim that in practice *migrants* refers to people who relocate by choice, usually for economic reasons. In other words, for some using *migrant* is a way to avoid prejudging claims to refugee status, while for others the use of *migrant* is its own prejudgment that implies the person being referred to is not a refugee.

A hard line on this subject was taken by English Al Jazeera on 20 August 2015, when it announced that it would no longer use the phrase "Mediterranean 'migrants'":

> The umbrella term *migrant* is no longer fit for purpose when it comes to describing the horror unfolding in the Mediterranean. It has evolved from its dictionary definitions into a tool that dehumanises and distances, a blunt pejorative....
>
> We become the enablers of governments who have political reasons for not calling those drowning in the Mediterranean what the majority of them are: refugees.[1]

Some other news organizations, however, are reluctant to embrace the word *refugee*. One argument is that refugee status is a legal question; as Tim Stanley of the *Daily Telegraph* argues,

---

1   Barry Malone, "Why Al Jazeera Will Not Say Mediterranean 'Migrants.'"

> The moment at which they can officially say
> whether they are refugees or economic migrants
> is the moment at which the EU state that is pro-
> cessing their claim makes its decision.[1]

The representatives of the British immigration law firm
Gherson, however, argue that in addition to its legal meaning *refugee* has a dictionary definition—one that applies to
anyone who has fled a country because of war or other
threats to safety—and "people can still meet the dictionary definition of 'refugee' irrespective of what their legal
status is."[2]

But even for those who acknowledge that some or even
most of the people in question can legitimately be described
as refugees, there is concern about oversimplification: if the
crisis involves some people fleeing serious and immediate
danger and some people seeking better economic pros-
pects, is it not better to use the more neutral term? This
is the stance adopted by Mark Memmott, Standards Editor
for NPR:

> Refugees leave their homes or their countries
> to escape persecution, or they might be seeking
> safety because of wars, as you said. Some may
> have been forced from their homes by armed
> forces. Certainly, many of the people who we've
> been hearing or reading about are refugees, but
> they've been coming from more than a dozen
> countries, and they've been coming for many

1   Quoted in Camilla Ruz, "The Battle over the Words Used to Describe
    Migrants," *BBC News Magazine*, 28 August 2015.
2   "Debate Erupts over Official Terminology—'Migrant Crisis' or 'Refugee Cri-
    sis'?," *Gherson Blog*, 4 September 2015.

political
controversies

different reasons; some of them maybe just to seek better lives. The word migrants fits for them all.[1]

Against arguments such as this, English Al Jazeera points out that, in fact, the UN has determined that "the overwhelming majority of these people are escaping war" (Malone); at what point is it misleading to use the blanket term "migrants" when most (though not all) of the people being described are refugees?

Without an easy solution to this controversy, conscientious writers strive to ensure that their language respects and highlights the humanity of the people involved and the gravity of their situations. David Marsh, a journalist for the *Guardian*, quotes his coworkers' views on the issue:

> One colleague who has been reporting extensively on the situation in Calais says: "The conclusion I came to was, wherever possible, to describe those in the camp as 'people' initially, with an extended phrase along the lines of 'more than 3,000 people who have fled war, poverty or persecution beyond Europe's borders....'"
>
> Another journalist says: "They are people—men, women and children, fathers and mothers, teachers and engineers, just like us—except they come from Syria, Eritrea, Afghanistan and elsewhere. Why not just call them 'people,' then list any other information we know that is relevant?"[2]

---

1   Quoted in Elizabeth Jensen, "'Refugee' Or 'Migrant': How to Refer to Those Fleeing Home," *NPR*, 21 August 2015.

2   "We Deride Them as 'Migrants.' Why Not Call Them People?," *The Guardian*, 28 August 2015.

Tar Sands? Oil Sands?

The years-long debate over the Keystone pipeline project brought to the attention of many Americans an issue that had already been part of the Canadian political landscape for decades: should the oil deposits in northern Alberta be referred to as the *tar sands* or the *oil sands*? The deposits are of an unusual sort; grains of sand are enveloped in bitumen, a viscous form of petroleum that resembles thick tar. Technically, it would be more accurate to refer to the *bituminous sands* of Alberta, but it's understandable that many prefer to use a term that's less of a mouthful.

Both available alternatives, however, are highly politicized; industry representatives and others who support the extraction of oil from these regions use the term *oil sands*; environmentalists and others who oppose it use the term *tar sands*.

The surprise is that the term the oil industry decided to use back in the 1920s was not *oil sands*; it was *tar sands*. From the 1920s until the mid-1960s the term *Alberta tar sands* was widely used—and the term *Alberta oil sands* was not used at all. It was not until around 1970 that use of the term *oil sands* became widespread; at that point the development of the area had started to become controversial, and some in the industry presumably began to feel that *oil sands* would sound more attractive than *tar sands*. Exactly what makes the image of oil sands more attractive than that of tar sands is not immediately clear; either way, we know the sand's not on a beach in the Mediterranean, and the oil's not from nearby olive trees. But for whatever reason, it seems that to most minds the word *oil* is less off-putting than the word *tar*. Perhaps the phrasing simply emphasizes that the sands are a source of oil, thus emphasizing the economic benefits of the oil industry—and downplaying the difficulty of extracting and processing oil from this sort of deposit. And perhaps the term *tar sands* is at least equally misleading, since the resource being extracted is not tar, but oil.

What term should you use if you'd like to remain impartial? Or if you support some bituminous sands projects but not others? Or if you don't want to get people's backs up on either side if you can help it?

One answer is to use the two terms *tar sands* and *oil sands* interchangeably—as was often done in the 1970s and 1980s by those with no axe to grind. Another is to use a term that more accurately names the substance involved: *bituminous sands*. It may be a bit of a mouthful, but it might still be the least awkward way to talk about the tar sands—or the oil sands—without immediately alienating a large portion of your audience.

Opposing Views on Publicly Naming Mass Murderers

Don's View:

John Hanlin is the sheriff of Douglas County, Oregon, where the mass murder of at least nine people took place in late September of 2015. Hanlin took an extraordinary stance after the killings:

> Let me be very clear: I will not name the shooter. I will not give him credit for this horrific act.... [I encourage the media to] avoid using [the shooter's name], repeating it, or engaging in any

> glorification and sensationalizing of him…. He in
> no way deserves it. Focus your attention on the
> victims and their families and helping them to
> recover.

It seems to me that Hanlin is right—and not only as a matter of what the shooter and his victims deserve. It's also a matter of deterring future such acts. As Doug Saunders and various others have pointed out, sensational acts of violence are often in large part motivated by a hope on the part of a mentally deranged person that the violent act will make him (it is almost always a him) famous.[1] The Oregon shooter was quite explicit about this. In the message he left for the world before committing his heinous act he commented on the perpetrator of the recent TV station murders in Virginia:

> I have noticed that people like him are all alone
> and unknown, yet when they spill a little blood,
> the whole world knows who they are…. Seems
> the more people you kill, the more you're in the
> limelight.

And we play right along. After reporting on Friday morning the sheriff's plea not to name the shooter, NPR named the shooter. In the front page article quoting the shooter's comments about killing people to get "in the limelight," *The New York Times* published his name and picture.

From the assassinations of a long line of politicians, to the 1989 École Polytechnique massacre, to the Columbine High School killings, to the Utøya Island mass murder in Norway in 2011, and through to the events in Oregon

---

1   See Saunders's article "Lone Wolf," *The Globe and Mail*, 25 October 2014.

mentioned above, we keep splashing the names and photos of the killers across our front pages and our television screens. Why can we not simply say, "The killer, whose name cannot be revealed, was a 26-year old man of mixed race with a history of instability and an avowed dislike of organized religion." No name, no photo, and no chance of becoming famous through committing deranged acts of violence. If news organizations feel they have a responsibility to dig deeper, fine. They can use a pseudonym such as "John Doe" if they need to; surely they have no true need to reveal the killer's name, or to publish his picture.

Our laws already recognize one important circumstance (youthful offenders) that we regard as providing sufficient justification to trump freedom-of-speech principles when it comes to revealing names; it's time to add another.

But even if legislators can't manage to change the laws governing media coverage, the media themselves can start to behave responsibly—to act in the way that Sheriff John Hanlin recommends, not in the way that the mass murderers are counting on.

Some will object that anyone determined to discover the identity of mass murderers will be able to do so—and of course that is true. But in practice very few of us possess such determination; if the media do not make these killers famous, they will not become famous—and those who kill in large part to become famous themselves will have lost their motivation.

Laura's View:

I can't deny that I find Don's argument immediately appealing: of course it is abhorrent that, when people commit atrocities, we respond just as they would have liked, by broadcasting their names, pictures, and manifestos in the media—often over and over again. Changing the way we report on mass killings seems to me clearly both a matter of good taste and a practical matter of discouraging future crimes, and I agree that we should circulate the names of (and images of) mass killers far less frequently than we do now. But would it be going too far to omit the name and image of the killer from public conversation altogether? There are, I think, some persuasive arguments that it would be.

As Don rightly points out, the kind of attention North American media pay to mass killers inspires other people who might commit such crimes to actually do so. Yes, repeating the names and sharing the photos of these killers as we currently do have deadly consequences—but the public discussion that involves their identities has concrete life-or-death consequences, too. We desperately need a public conversation about how to prevent mass killings in North America, and such a conversation will necessarily involve a discussion of what motivated the killers, as well as what might have stopped them. As reporter Garrett Haake argues,

> By choosing not to name mass killers, journalists abdicate responsibility for asking and answering deeper questions about why an event took place, and what could have been done to stop it. Was the killer mentally ill? How did he (for the killers are nearly always men) acquire a weapon? Why did he target who he targeted? Who knew about

the plot and what steps, if any, did they take to stop it? What signs were missed?[1]

One example Haake gives is that of public conversation surrounding Dylann Roof, who murdered several members of the congregation at a Charleston church. The wide circulation of a photo in which he poses with a gun and a Confederate flag led to a public debate about the flag's status as a racist symbol—and to the flag's eventual removal from the South Carolina Capitol grounds. Erik Wemple of *The Washington Post* offers another example of discussion of a mass killer's identity leading to a concrete policy change: the release of the mental health records of Seung-Hui Cho, responsible for the 2007 murders at Virginia Tech.[2] Senator Jim Webb introduced an amendment to clarify the application of the Family Educational Rights and Privacy Act, claiming that Cho's records suggested that the massacre could have "been prevented had the policy been more clear on when information about a mentally ill student can be shared by a university."[3]

Don suggests that we can accomplish the same sort of discussion while avoiding using the actual names of killers. Is this really true? I'd argue that, when it comes to matters of political importance, it is most effective to name things clearly and directly. If I refer to the serial murder of sex workers in Vancouver's Downtown East Side, that's wordy—and, unfortunately, since sex workers in Vancouver continually face all kinds of dangers, it's also a little unclear. But if I refer to the Pickton murders, which are famous

---

1 "Why We Name the Shooters," *WUSA*, 2 October 2015.
2 "Media: Please Ignore Oregon Sheriff's Appeal Never to Mention Shooter's Name," 2 October 2015.
3 Emily Freidman, "Va. Tech Shooter Seung-Hui Cho's Mental Health Records Released," *ABC News*, 19 August 2009.

across Canada, what I am talking about is immediately clear, and I can move on to a discussion of policy (in this case, for example, the fact that the murders were allowed to continue for decades before any adequate police investigation was undertaken). An added benefit to clearly and directly naming killers is that people who know them are enabled to come forward—perhaps with useful information that police, journalists, and policy-makers would not be able to obtain otherwise.

There is another practical consideration at play here: if we don't make public the identities of mass killers, will the public simply make something up to fill the hole in public knowledge? Evidence suggests that they will—and often in a way that carries an unfortunate racial or religious charge. In the case of the Douglas County shooter whose identity John Hanlin refused to report, false rumors circulated that the killer was a Muslim.[1] Perhaps in that case, identifying the killer as "a 26-year old mixed-race man with an avowed dislike of organized religion" could ameliorate that effect, but there seems something dangerous, too, in foregrounding a killer's race and/or religion without attaching it to an individual identity. As we discuss in the main text, when a member of a marginalized group commits a mass killing, it already provokes a backlash of violence and discrimination against ordinary members of that group. If ordinary Muslims are already painted with the same brush as Omar Mateen (the killer of a large number of people in an Orlando nightclub in 2016), how much more harm would it do if the Pulse shooter were discussed in the media not as a specific individual but as "an Islamic man of Afghan background"?

1   Mark Follman, "How the Media Inspires Mass Shooters," *Mother Jones*, 6 October 2015.

And would Mateen have cared whether he became famous by name or famous as "the Pulse shooter"? I very much doubt it. There are other, more important changes we could make to avoid glorifying mass killers.[1] For example, Reid Meloy, a forensic psychologist with a focus on mass killers, suggests that we "rethink" some of the language we use surrounding the act of mass killing itself:

> "Stop using the term 'lone wolf' and stop using 'school shooter,'" he says. "In the minds of young men this makes these acts of violence cool. They think, 'This has got some juice behind it, and I can get out there and do something really cool—I can be a lone wolf. I can be a shooter.'" Instead, Meloy suggests using terms such as "an act of lone terrorism" and "an act of mass murder."[2]

We can also be more thoughtful about the kinds of representation we give, limiting, for example, the direct quotation of killers' manifestos and the circulation of the posed "pseudocommando" photos they often leave behind. And we can limit the repetition of killers' names beyond what is actually necessary to a productive public conversation. The key, I would argue, is to use the names thoughtfully and responsibly—not to avoid using them at all.

---

1   See Follman's article in *Mother Jones* for an in-depth discussion of these and other recommendations.
2   Quoted in Follman.

Questions and Suggestions for Discussion

1. Using the Ngram viewer,[1] compare (and comment on) the frequency of use of the expressions *pro-life* and *pro-choice* between 1960 and 2008.

2. Using the Ngram viewer, compare (and comment on) the frequency of use of the terms *illegal immigrant* and *undocumented immigrant* between 1920 and 2008.

3. Using the Ngram viewer, compare (and comment on) the frequency of use of the terms *oil sands* and *tar sands* between 1850 and 2008.

4. Explore the etymology of the terms *gunman* and *shooter*, and (using the Ngram viewer) compare (and comment on) the frequency with which the two terms were used between 1500 and 2008.

5. Using the Ngram viewer, compare (and comment on) the relative frequency of use of the phrases *I'm fat*, *she's fat*, and *he's fat* in 2008.

political controversies

---

1   For a quick introduction to the Ngram viewer, see the section entitled "How to Use This Book" at the beginning of the volume.

SERIOUSNESS & HUMOR, EUPHEMISM & PLAIN SPEAKING

It's often felt that all the issues we are asked to take account of in speaking and writing about gender, race, religion, sexual orientation, and disability create, in aggregate, something of an oppressive atmosphere—that we are forced to tread on our toes all the time in the name of "political correctness," that we can't speak plainly, and that we're being asked to give up our sense of humor. It's true that there are serious issues involved, and that trying not to disparage people different from ourselves can take a fair bit of thought and a fair bit of effort. In that respect it's not a lot different from the rest of life. It can take a fair bit of thought and a fair bit of effort to be courteous and tactful to our relatives, or to people in our school or at our place of work who are from backgrounds quite similar to our own. And yet we manage—and we manage to express our sense of humor, too.

We do have to acknowledge that there are restrictions in what it's appropriate to say or do—just as we have to acknowledge that the conventions of acceptable behavior impose restrictions when it comes to what we can say to our parents and grandparents, and how we refer to them. Not least of all, we are obliged to accept some restrictions on certain forms of humor. It's often suggested by well-meaning opponents of racism, sexism, and so on that racist and sexist jokes are never truly funny. But that's just not true; if it were not possible for humans to find humor in racist and sexist jokes and comments, no one would ever have laughed at them. One of the saddest things about the human species is that our sense of humor is far from an unqualified good; we are all too easily amused by jokes about those who are less powerful than we are, or who are simply different from us.

We should, then, be prepared *not* to make some jokes, even if they really are funny, and *not* to comment in certain ways, even if we know that the comment is sure to get a laugh. We should, as we grow up (and for some of us this takes longer than for others[1]), be prepared to put other values ahead of *getting a laugh*. But does that mean we have to give up our sense of humor? Not at all. We don't even have to give up humor that's about gender or race or religion or sexual orientation. What we should be prepared to give up is humor that's based on contempt and superciliousness, humor that comes at the expense of those less privileged than ourselves, humor that comes at the expense of those who have done nothing to deserve it. Let's look at a comparative example:

> Three religious leaders are comparing notes on how they deal with the funds that have been donated to their institutions during services.
>
> "Well, I have a system that seems to work pretty well," says one. Of course my institution is a place of God, and when people donate money they expect that it will be for God's work. But I have various expenses, and I could not do God's work myself without receiving some recompense. This

---

1   One of the authors wishes to take this opportunity to acknowledge that he was well into his twenties before he started to realize that jokes about "Personitoba" (see above) were neither as pointed nor as funny as he had previously thought. [DL]

is the system that I have found works best: I draw a line on the floor, and from a point on that line I throw the entire amount donated that week into the air. What lands on one side of the line is for God's work; what lands on the other side of the line is my own compensation."

"How funny!" says the second religious leader. "I have a very similar system. I draw a circle on the floor, and from any point on the circumference of that circle I throw the entire amount donated that week into the air. What lands inside the circle is for God; what lands outside is my own compensation."

"This is truly extraordinary!" says the third religious leader. "We all three of us have very similar systems. The way I do things is almost precisely the same. Of course everyone takes a somewhat different approach when it comes to the specifics. My own approach this: I throw the entire amount donated that week into the air—and what God wants, he keeps."

This is a joke that has been told in slightly different ways for decades, almost always with the three leaders identified as belonging to a particular religious group—Catholics, Scottish Presbyterians, Muslims, Jews, whoever. Told that way, it becomes a joke that is in part at least against a particular religion; however funny it may be, it is surely an example of humor that is objectionable. Told in the way it is set out above, on the other hand, with no religions specified, it becomes a joke about selfishness and greed, and about how humans are all too often able to rationalize their selfishness and greed.

What about race? Again, let's look at a case in point:

> Just a few years before Barack Obama's ascent to
> the White House, few people imagined that in 2008
> America would be ready to elect as their president
> someone who was sort-of African American.

Is this one-liner a case of appropriate humor on the subject
of race? Surely the answer is yes. It's perhaps in part a joke
about Obama's unusual background. But more importantly,
it's a joke about the *degree* to which America was ready in
2008 to elect a Black president; as was widely discussed at
the time, many Americans who would have been reluctant
to vote for someone as Black as Obama's father were quite
prepared to vote for someone whose parentage was half
Black, half white.

We should perhaps not leave the subject of humor without acknowledging that efforts to insist on bias-free language can legitimately be the butt of humor too. Here's a
dialogue among three characters with unusual names:

> *Unthinking*: That's really gay!
> *Thinking*: Could you could put that in a different
> way? "That's so gay" is an expression that really is
> hurtful to gay people.
> *Unthinking*: What I mean is, that's really stupid.
> *Overthinking*: I'm afraid that what you've just said
> could be regarded as offensive by anyone who's
> ever done anything stupid.

If humor is consistent with doing one's best to take ethical
considerations into account in one's speaking and writing,
so too is plain speaking. A great many people feel that striving to make the language we use free of bias is likely to result

in euphemism and silliness—and that, for that reason, it's not worth the effort. Absurd examples such as "vertically challenged" are put forward again and again as if they were the typical products of any striving for bias-free language; in fact, such euphemisms are seriously recommended by almost no one. That's not to say that ongoing efforts to speak and write fairly about other groups have not resulted in some absurdity, and some euphemistic language. To be sure, they have—and in some of those cases the euphemisms may have been unfortunate. But anyone who wishes to take issue with the use of a euphemism such as *mentally challenged* should on the same grounds take issue with other forms of euphemism—most certainly including euphemisms of a truly horrific sort that are sometimes used by some who style themselves as opponents of "political correctness." Former American Vice President Dick Cheney, who oversaw the American government's use of interrogation techniques during the administration of George W. Bush, is an example of just such a person. Cheney has attacked others for using euphemisms rather than speaking plainly. But how does he refer to the practice of repeatedly subjecting prisoners to extreme pain? He calls it "enhanced interrogation of high-value detainees." A wide range of impartial authorities have concluded that the "waterboarding" and other techniques practiced by the American military under Cheney's oversight were, quite simply, forms of torture. Republican Senator John McCain, who underwent torture himself during the Vietnam war, has said exactly that quite unequivocally—and not just about waterboarding: "you can't claim that tying someone to the floor and having them freeze to death is not torture.... What [Americans] need to do is come clean, move forward, and vow never to do it again." Dick Cheney will have none of that; he continues to insist on euphemism. Asked when he appeared on 14 December 2014 on NBC's *Meet the Press*, he was adamant about "what we did with respect to enhanced interrogation."

Like many others, some politicians will doubtless never learn how to be good with words.

A CASE TO CONSIDER

Opposing Views on Race and Comedy: The Case of Amy Schumer

Don's View:

The jokes comedian Amy Schumer used to tell about Hispanics received a lot of attention in 2015. Were they funny? Were they racist? Were they in some way jokes against racism? In *The Washington Post* Stacey Patton and David J. Leonard argued unequivocally that some of Schumer's jokes about Hispanic people were racist—as did Monica Heisey in *The Guardian*.[1] Among the many who leapt to her defence was David Sims, writing in *The Atlantic*:

> You could micro-analyze every joke Schumer has told, good and bad, but that would undermine the value of the experimental nature of stand-up, which lives in the split moment an audience decides to—or not to—laugh.[2]

---

1 See Patton and Leonard, "Don't Believe Her Defenders. Amy Schumer's Jokes Are Racist," *The Washington Post*, 6 July 2015; and Heisey, "Amy Schumer: Comedy's Viral Queen," *The Guardian*, 28 June 2015.
2 David Sims, "Amy Schumer and the Growing Pains of Comedy," *The Atlantic*, 30 June 2015.

Not only does Sims not microanalyze any of Schumer's allegedly racist jokes; he doesn't even tell us what they were. Is microanalysis really such a bad thing? Let's try some.

Perhaps it's best to start with one of Schumer's jokes that seems relatively defensible:

> Nothing works 100 percent of the time, except Mexicans.

What is this joke taking aim at? It draws on a stereotype of Mexicans. This may be a stereotype that portrays them in a positive light—as extremely hardworking—but even supposedly positive stereotypes are still stereotypes, and if this joke does no more than that, that's definitely a problem. Of course there's more to it than that. By phrasing the opening to the joke as "*Nothing* works ..." rather than as "*Nobody* works ...," Schumer suggests an analogy between Mexican workers and machines. So who is the target of the joke? Surely it's the people who treat underpaid workers from Mexico as machines—whether they be owners of California fruit farms or wealthy families employing Hispanic workers to clean the house and take care of the children. Behind the image of Mexicans working "100 percent of the time" is the implication that Mexican workers in the United States are exploited, that the economic system forces many to work multiple jobs and/or to accept inhumanly long shifts. In this case, we would argue, Schumer's joke works more to undermine racism than to reinforce it.

It's hard not to see Schumer's joke about Latina jealousy, though, as anything but flat-out racist:

> So many great movies, this year. *Gone Girl* ... how
> good was *Gone Girl*, you guys? Such a good movie.
> If you didn't see it, it's the story of what one
> crazed white woman—or all Latinas—do if you
> cheat on them. That's a fact.

What does Amy Dunne—the "crazed white woman" in
Gone Girl—do in the movie? Frame her cheating husband
for murder and commit a grisly murder herself, among
other preposterous acts. Schumer, then, is suggesting that
evil manifestations of extreme jealousy—so rare among
white women as to mark Amy Dunne as "crazed"—are
universal among women of Latin American background.
Even worse was this joke:

> I used to date Hispanic guys, but now I prefer
> consensual.

In this case, the obvious implication is that "Hispanic guys"
are rapists.

Schumer's initial defense was that when she does stand-
up comedy "I go in and out of playing an irreverent idiot.
That includes making dumb jokes involving race."[1] Later,
however, she said that she had stopped telling "jokes like
that," that she was "taking responsibility," that she hoped
she hadn't hurt anyone, and that she apologized if she
had. Many commentators were clearly of the view that
no apology was necessary—that comedy about touchy
subjects such as race is legitimate, and that the jokes in
question represented no more than a comedian pushing
the envelope while in character. Sims, for example, while

---

1   The jokes are quoted in Alex Abad-Santos, "Amy Schumer's Comedy Is Smart
     on Feminism: Is It Bad on Race?" *Vox*, 1 July 2015; they are also available as
     video clips at several locations online.

acknowledging that the jokes in question were "clunky" and "not that well-crafted or funny," argues that "it's unfair and impossible to ask a comedian to push boundaries without also giving them room to write material that sometimes falls short or pushes too hard."

Like Sims, most of Schumer's defenders on this issue do not quote the actual jokes themselves. And like him, they tend as well to frame the issue in general terms, as one involving comedy and the topic of race, not as one that involves jokes about Hispanics specifically. Typical is Debra Kessler, writing on the blog Interrobang:

> [P]erformed comedy that integrates and confronts, and yes even "plays with" race and bias, is not the same as a "chicken and watermelon and pickaninny joke." There is nuance and skill that performers use to communicate that they are not advocating racism and intolerance—on the contrary, they believe in inclusion and tolerance.[1]

By all means watch the video clip yourself; in our view it strains credulity to imagine that the relevant part of Schumer's stand-up routine at the MTV Movie Awards is being delivered so as to suggest a persona that Schumer herself intends us to criticize. So far as the content of the jokes is concerned, Kessler evidently regards a "chicken and watermelon and pickaninny joke" as unacceptable—whereas "jokes" that all Latinas are demonically jealous or that all Hispanic guys are rapists are examples of comedy that "integrates and confronts ... race and bias." Is there in fact any difference between the two? Perhaps the only real

---

1   Debra Kessler, "*Washington Post* Writer Who Accused Amy Schumer of Racism Never Saw Her Standup or TV Show," *The Interrobang*, 10 July 2015.

difference is this: America now has a decades-long tradition of acknowledging the inappropriateness of jokes directed against Black people (whether a comedian delivers them "in character" or not)—and does not yet have the same tradition of sensitivity when it comes to racist jokes about Hispanics.

And let's not fool ourselves that this sort of joke is challenging the audience or taking issue with racism itself; such comedy does nothing of the kind. If a comedian truly wants to challenge the audience in those sorts of ways, it's easy to imagine how it can be done. You take aim at the racist views, not at the people who are the victims of racism.

Should we try to outlaw the type of joke Amy Schumer used to tell? Definitely not: any attempt to impose censorship of that sort would likely do more harm than good. But should we acknowledge such humor as racist, and criticize it on those grounds? Yes, absolutely. And is it a good thing that Schumer stopped telling that sort of joke, and apologized? Yes, absolutely. Do we all make mistakes, and learn from them? Let's hope so!

Laura's View:

When it comes to the controversy regarding Amy Schumer's racially charged jokes, as Don points out, most of Schumer's defenders don't quote the jokes in question or subject them to thorough analysis. But this doesn't necessarily mean that the jokes can't stand up to this sort of examination. Let's take another look at the *Gone Girl* joke:

> So many great movies, this year. *Gone Girl* ... how good was *Gone Girl*, you guys? Such a good movie.

> If you didn't see it, it's the story of what one crazed white woman—or all Latinas—do if you cheat on them. That's a fact.

It's easy to see that the stereotype of the "crazy Latina" is extremely offensive, and if all this joke does is perpetuate such a stereotype, then it is unquestionably an unethical joke. But *is* that all it does? Though not all critics have seen it this way,[1] *Gone Girl* is arguably a misogynist film in which the character of Amy Dunne embodies all the worst stereotypes about women: she makes false claims regarding rape, manipulates her husband into remaining in their marriage against his will, and generally passes herself off as a victim when in reality she victimizes the men in her life. Another way to understand Schumer's *Gone Girl* joke is that it draws attention to the negative stereotypes perpetuated in the movie by linking them to the stereotype of the "crazy Latina"—a more obvious manifestation of the misogynist views behind the character of Amy Dunne herself. At the same time, the joke shows that women of color are even more strongly affected by such misogyny than white women are. In this reading, "That's a fact" serves to provide ironic emphasis, suggesting that *neither* stereotype is anywhere near factual.

What about the "Hispanic guys" joke?

> I used to date Hispanic guys, but now I prefer consensual.

---

[1] For an alternative view, see Roxane Gay's reading of the book upon which the film was based, in which Gay celebrates Amy Dunne as a rare exception in an age of "likeable" heroines ("Not Here to Make Friends," Buzzfeed, 3 January 2014).

To understand what commentary is intended here, it may help to situate this joke in the broader context of Schumer's career—something that, notably, many of her critics have not done. (Stacey Patton, for example, co-author of the article "Don't Believe Her Defenders. Amy Schumer's Jokes Are Racist," admitted to never having watched a full set of Schumer's stand-up or any of her sketch comedy.[1]) In her sketch comedy show, *Inside Amy Schumer*, Schumer frequently plays an unpleasant New York woman who is oblivious to her own privilege and prejudice. In one sketch, her attitude causes God (played by Paul Giamatti) to mutter to himself, "I really need to stop making so many white girls"; in another sketch, set in an Urban Outfitters, Schumer's character is paralyzed by discomfort as she tries to identify the Black sales associate who helped her without mentioning his skin color, but is also so blinded by her racism that she is unable to distinguish him from the other Black associates in the store.[2] This context gives credence to Schumer's explanation that in her stand-up routines she sometimes plays "an irreverent idiot" who makes "dumb jokes involving race"; she plays a variation of the same character in these sketches.

What happens if we consider the "Hispanic guys" joke in the context of this persona? The joke comments on two things: the culture of sexual consent and the stereotype of Hispanic men as rapists. Arguably, the phrase "now I prefer consensual" suggests that the stand-up persona Schumer has adopted in this routine is that of a woman blinded by

---

1   See Debra Kessler, "Washington Post Writer Who Accused Amy Schumer of Racism Never Saw Her Standup or TV Show."

2   In her critique of Schumer, Heisey interprets this sketch differently, claiming that the "problem appears to be that all the store's black employees look the same"; Sims rightly points out that "the joke there is on Schumer."

her culture's prejudices to the point that she doesn't understand consent as more than a "preference." If this persona is wrong about sexual consent, might she be wrong about race, too? Undoubtedly, this joke is meant to be absurd and to make audiences uncomfortable—precisely because it draws attention to false beliefs in North American culture about rape *and* about racist stereotypes.

The context of the rest of Schumer's work makes it clear that her intentions are to attack racism through comedy (at least to the extent that an artist's intentions can be clear). But good intention by itself is not an excuse—and even if these jokes are intended to undermine racist beliefs, it is still a problem if they fail to actually do so. E. Alex Jung, writing for *Vulture*, points out that when Schumer plays the racist, unlikeable "dumb girl" character in her sketch comedy, that character's flaws are revealed in her interactions with other characters:

> These sketches work because there's another voice to counteract Schumer's. But in her stand-up, there isn't any pushback: The joke is simply whatever the "dumb girl" says it is.[1]

I would argue that at least some of the burden is on Schumer's audience to provide this pushback—to be on the lookout for ironic or uncomfortable statements, and to interpret those statements critically. But there is also a burden on Schumer herself to lead audiences partway there.

There is, however, another way in which humor about race is not trivial. Humor is "a safe vehicle" for racism because comedy offers a way for human beings to engage

---

1   See "Why Amy Schumer Reacted to Criticism of Her Race Jokes Like a Stand-up—and Why That's a Dead End," 29 June 2015.

with ideas that make us uncomfortable—and the same characteristic makes humor an important tool for those who want to question and dismantle racist ideologies. New Yorker critic Emily Nussbaum has praised Schumer's ability to make political points in her comedy without becoming "didactic—or worse, smug."[1] Schumer is able to help her audience negotiate important ideas—and to keep that audience watching—in part because her comedy is not always straightforward, and it trusts audiences to respond thoughtfully rather than leading them by the hand.

Patton and Leonard rightly remind us that a joke is never "*just* a joke,'" and yes, humor is powerful, but that is exactly why we need comics to tackle issues of race. Let's return to Sims's assertion that

> it's unfair and impossible to ask a comedian to push boundaries without also giving them room to write material that sometimes falls short or pushes too hard.

This looks like a claim in defense of thoughtless racism, but it's not. It's a claim that if western culture is to progress in the direction of less racism and more inclusivity, we need artists—and especially comedians—from all backgrounds to engage with race in complex and engaging ways. We even need them to take risks that will inevitably produce offensive material some of the time.

It would be wonderful if all jokes against racism were in no way open to misinterpretation—except that with all the irony and ambiguity removed it would be hard to imagine those jokes being funny. This doesn't mean that anything

1   "The Little Tramp," 11 May 2015.

goes; what comics do should be as open to criticism as anything else, and people should always speak up if they feel attempts at humor to be inappropriate or irresponsible. Some comedians' attempts at humor do cross a line, and they should be called on it when that happens. But if, as Sims reports, Schumer has now eliminated race-related jokes from her stand-up routines, that's a shame.

POLITICALLY CORRECT:
A HISTORY & COMMENTARY

For those with a sense of history, the phrase *politically correct* conjures up images of the totalitarian states of the mid-twentieth century—the sort of thing that Stalin's show trials of the 1930s epitomized, and that George Orwell satirized in the novels *Animal Farm* and *1984*. But the term itself seems hardly to have been used in English before 1970, when it started to make its appearance in Marxist and anti-imperialist writings. In such contexts it was employed in utmost seriousness:

> On the one hand we should demand that the poet's work conform to the correct political tendency; on the other hand we have the right to expect that his work be of high quality....[1]

> With Pan-Africanism as a political base, Guinea is a dangerous nation to Portuguese interests in Guinea-Bissau.... [A]s a politically correct and politically advancing state, Guinea will make a dangerous neighbor [for a Portuguese colony].[2]

The term did not begin to gain wider currency until the 1980s—by which time it had lost most of its seriousness. The oldest of this book's three authors first heard *politically correct* used by George Kirkpatrick, who later became Broadview Press's second employee and went on

---

1   Walter Benjamin (translated by John Heckman), "The Author as Producer," *New Left Review*, vol. 1, no. 62, July–August 1970.
2   Nancy Irving, "Guinea and Imperialism," *The Harvard Crimson*, 15 December 1970.

to a distinguished career as a freelance book designer. In 1985 he had just opened a small shop that sold used books of the academic and literary sort. If you asked him whether he hoped to profit from the bookstore he would give you a pleasant, ironic smile and say that it would be nice to make a living wage from the shop, but that to use the word *profit* might be considered politically incorrect.

That was the sort of context in which the term began to become common currency in 1980s North American culture. It was used more frequently about political economy than about culture. It was used almost always with some degree of irony. And it was used almost exclusively by people whose politics were progressive but who were non-doctrinaire, and who enjoyed poking gentle fun at some of their fellow travelers on the political left who were rather more serious, and rather more doctrinaire.

How quickly things changed once more. Within a decade *politically correct* had come to be used with greater frequency still, and in a very different way. By the late 1990s *politically correct* (and the compound noun *political correctness*) had become a weapon—a term of abuse hurled by those on the right of center against those on the left. And that remains the most common context in which *politically correct* and *political correctness* are used. Here's an example from a 2012 article in *The Washington Times*, published under the title "Leftists' Politically Correct Dictionary":

> Since the 1960s, a "correct" political language has been imposed on Americans.
> For example, none of the following set of terms was in the *New Webster Encyclopedic Dictionary of the English Language* in 1971: African-American,

> entitlement, environmentalism, Hispanic, multiculturalism, Native American, nonjudgmental, sexism, victimization. Just 15 years later, all of these leftist terms were in *Webster's New World Collegiate Dictionary* of 1986....
>
> Left-wing activists have seen to it that students entering universities receive lists of forbidden words, such as the use of "man" in generic reference to human beings (for example, the word "congressman" for any member of Congress, which is said to be an affront to women). Those lists provide substitute diction for the censored words (e.g. "freshperson" for freshman).... The widespread use of politically correct language is "deconstructing" American culture. Our shared belief in God-given, equal birthrights to life, liberty and the pursuit of happiness is being destroyed, along with belief in constitutional government, Judeo-Christian morality, marriage, the free market and personal responsibility.[1]

In attacks such as this the sarcastic use of the word "correct" acts as a substitute for any actual argument as to whether the terms are more or less appropriate than the ones they are intended to replace. The writer jumps to a grand ideological assertion without ever coming to grips with any of the specifics. And what of the assertion that this sort of language has been *imposed* on Americans? The only evidence provided of the supposed imposition is that the words McElroy cites were added to the dictionary over the fifteen-year

---

1   John Harmon McElroy, "Leftists' Politically Correct Dictionary," *The Washington Times*, 15 October 2012.

period in question. Were there any laws passed to prevent people from saying *congressman* rather than *congressperson*? Of course not. Since the mid-twentieth century dictionaries have tended overwhelmingly to be descriptive rather than prescriptive; as language changes, a new edition will inform readers that an old term is "now widely considered inappropriate in formal English," or "now considered offensive by many." No dictionary nowadays attempts to impose linguistic change.

But what of the notion that students entering university "receive lists of forbidden words"? One cannot vouch for all individual instructors, of course, but one can check the textbooks that they have chosen. Typical of the late 1980s is Dornan and Dawe's then-popular *Brief English Handbook*. This is the closest that textbook comes to a list of "forbidden words":

> Changes are taking place in American English usage that reflect a growing awareness of sexism in American society. These changes affect what some social critics describe as a masculine bias embedded in our language.... Using recent coinages can help you avoid sounding biased. For instance, you can replace *chairman*, which in the recent past was used to refer to both men and women, with *chairwoman* when a woman holds the position and with *chairperson* when the person's gender is unknown.[1]

1   Edward A. Dornan and Charles W. Dawe, *The Brief English Handbook*, 3e, Addison Wesley, 1990. Note that the English language has developed further in the past decades; now, *chair* is used in reference to people of all genders.

politically correct

That's about as doctrinaire as it gets in the textbooks of the late 1980s. By the twenty-first century the language is a little stronger—but not much more so:

> Using non-sexist language is a matter of courtesy—of respect for and sensitivity to the feelings of others.... The nouns *man* and *men* were once used to refer generically to persons of either sex. Current usage demands gender-neutral terms for references to both men and women.[1]

Even in the twenty-first century, then, the leading writing handbook advises only that "current usage demands gender-neutral terms"—not that students are strictly prohibited from using a word such as *chairman*.[2] The tendency of progressive textbooks, then, (and, as we'll see in a moment, not all textbooks have been progressive) has all along been to provide no more than gentle guidelines. But perhaps the suggestion is that most university instructors have been going far beyond the textbook's guidelines in the strength of their recommendations on these points—absolutely insisting that students stop saying *freshman* and *congressman*. If that is the case, they are having remarkably little success. Ngrams indicate that, while *chair* is now used more frequently than *chairman* (with the clunky *chairperson* a distant third), *flight attendant* did not overtake *stewardess* in

---

1   Diana Hacker and Nancy Sommers, *A Writer's Reference*, 5e, Bedford/St. Martin's, 2002.
2   There is, you may notice, a glossary at the end of this book that we suppose could be considered a list of "forbidden words." We hope you won't take it that way, but rather, like the rest of this book, as a list of guidelines you can use to help you approach language in a more inclusive, less biased way. Our hope is that, if this book affects your writing, it will be by encouraging you to think more critically about the language you use—not by imposing laws for you to blindly obey.

frequency of use until the late 1990s—and even now *stewardess* is used almost as frequently. *Congressmen* continues to be used more than ten times as frequently as *congressional representatives*, and *freshmen* more than five times more frequently than *first-year students*.[1] So much for the "imposition" of "politically correct" language on America. The fact is that Americans, Canadians, and others around the world are slowly but steadily moving towards more inclusive habits of language not because some left-wing cabal is imposing the change on them, but because when the specific issues are fully and fairly discussed, more and more people see the sense of using language that may help make the world a fairer and better place.

What about the issue of euphemism? It is often claimed that those striving for inclusive or gender-neutral language go to ridiculous lengths to avoid giving offense—and that has indeed occasionally happened. In most cases, though, the complaints that are made as to the supposed euphemistic excesses of political correctness turn out to be entirely spurious:

> We've been exhorted to abandon *deaf, dumb*, and *blind* for *aurally, verbally*, and *visually challenged*. Time will tell whether these confections become part of the living language, although it's hard to see what purpose they serve other than to obscure the truth.… American English has developed a taste for euphemisms which are little better than lies.… When assessing the merits of politically correct

---

1   *Freshpersons* has never, so far as we are aware, been seriously suggested as an alternative to freshmen; like many who attack the left on these sorts of grounds, McElroy has simply made up a ludicrous-sounding example.

politically correct

English, one should bear in mind that America
is the county that adopted the words *rooster* and
donkey because it couldn't cope with the implications of *cock* and *ass*.[1]

Much as these authors amusingly distinguish between
American and British linguistic history, their complaints as
to "politically correct English" are very much the same as
those that conservative American commentators have made
repeatedly over the years. But *are* we in fact being asked to
replace the word *deaf* with *aurally challenged*? Not at all. On
the contrary, terms such as *aurally challenged* and *hearing
impaired* are a point of contention for members of the Deaf
community, most of whom object to them in part for their
euphemistic qualities. Even those who use *aurally challenged*
as a blanket term to refer to all those who are hard of hearing to any extent generally do not shy away from also using
terms such as *deaf* and *partially deaf*. In similar fashion,
blind and *visually impaired* have distinct meanings—one
can be visually impaired without being blind—and no one
has suggested we eliminate *blind* from the language. (The
word *dumb*, for what should be obvious reasons, is a special
case here.) In short, the objection raised here to "politically
correct" language in general turns out to apply only to a very
few instances.

Where supposed euphemisms are concerned, many conservative writers seem so determined to find awkwardness and
absurdity in inclusive and gender-neutral language that they
repeatedly invent "politically correct" coinages themselves in
order to secure themselves a target. Here's a textbook example:

---

1   Elizabeth Bartsch-Parker, Stephen Burger, and Roibeard O'Maolalaigh, *Lonely
     Planet British Phrasebook*, 1999.

Maintaining Objectivity
Avoiding discriminating language is important.
Just as important, however, is avoiding a witch
hunt. Taken to extremes, political correctness will
weaken your writing. *Middleman*, for example, is
a perfectly legitimate term, widely understood.
There is no point in confusing readers by substi-
tuting *distributional intermediary* merely to avoid
the suffix -*man*. Little is gained by referring to a
stripper as an *ecdysiast* when most readers will not
recognize the euphemism. And no one is going
to take seriously a writer who calls short people
vertically challenged. Remember, the point of considerate language is to be fair and polite, not to be
obscure or silly.[1]

Think about this for only a moment, and it may seem quite
unexceptionable—entirely reasonable, even. Think again.
The tip-off here is the way that the question of the word
middleman has been approached: not as the occasion for an
interesting, if possibly difficult, search for ways of expressing ourselves that will avoid both awkwardness and bias,
but rather as a matter that will inevitably involve a choice
between the two. The authors here seem more interested in
finding reasons to ridicule the struggle for fairness than in
joining in the effort to improve things.

Let's approach the word *middleman* in a different frame
of mind. To start with, the fair comparison is not between
distributional intermediary and *middleman* but between
intermediary and *middleman*. Perhaps the former is more
awkward, but it is not obviously so:

---

1   Bonnie Carter and Craig Skates, *The Rinehart Guide to Grammar and Style*,
     4e, Rinehart, 1996.

- One of the reasons for high prices in this industry is that there are too many middlemen.
- One of the reasons for high prices in this industry is that there are too many intermediaries.

Alternatives in different circumstances may include *wholesalers, distributors, go-betweens*—none of them obscure, confusing, or laughable. *Ecdysiast* is indeed a laughable euphemism, but not one that is needed to circumvent biased usages. (*He's a male stripper* suffers from the same defect as *He's a male nurse*, but *stripper* in itself is gender-neutral.) And, though there is indeed a societal bias against short people, no one seriously suggests that the euphemism *vertically challenged* is a solution.

When writers of this persuasion use the term "politically correct," they also often suggest that they themselves have no political agenda; they are "maintaining objectivity," as the authors of the above passage style it. Notice in this connection that the authors of *The Rinehart Guide* couch the matter as an issue of etiquette rather than one of equity: "the point of considerate language is to be fair and polite." To be sure, it is a virtue to be polite and considerate. But unquestioning politeness to those in positions of power and privilege may sometimes entail an acceptance of terms of reference that are anything but fair. Sometimes one may have to choose between being fair and being polite. And the point of searching for inclusive or gender-neutral ways of expressing oneself is in fact not to be polite, but to be fair. Sometimes it comes down to a choice; language can be an instrument of positive change, or an instrument of repression. In that context we can probably never avoid

politically correct

being biased in one direction or the other, and we are wise to remember that complete objectivity is impossible.

Regrettably, the prevailing tack taken by those fighting against inclusive or gender-neutral language has remained mockery rather than argument. Thus, for example, columnist Ron Haggart mocked efforts to replace the term *manhole cover* by suggesting as an alternative *circular utility access alternative facilitative infrastructure*.[1] Ha ha. The most commonly proposed alternative to *manhole*, of course, is nothing so awkward or absurd. Moreover, *sewer hole* more accurately describes the object in question; someone new to English would surely never be able to guess the meaning of *manhole* from its component parts. (Indeed, the word might lead to embarrassing misunderstandings.)

None of this should be taken to suggest that there are not awkwardnesses to struggle with in the search for appropriate means of expression. (*Statesman*, for example, resists any easy substitutions.) But the awkwardnesses are surprisingly few. *Chair* and *flight attendant* felt a little odd at first, but few are bothered by them now. *First-year student* still feels odd to many Americans, but not in Canada, where it has always been used. And the process can and should continue.[2] One of the authors of this book had assumed that *sportship* would somehow make an awkward substitute for *sportsmanship*—until he heard former Olympian Abby Hoffman on the radio, speaking quite naturally of the sportship of certain athletes at the Rio Olympics.

---

1   Ron Haggart, "That Covers It," *The Globe and Mail*, 19 March 2004.
2   The process can be free-spirited and entertaining as well as serious. As a gender-neutral alternative to *snowman*, for example, we'd suggest that *snowbody* (rhymes with *nobody*) is worthy of consideration; perhaps that new coinage will never catch on, but it's worth noting that there are few things more gender-neutral than a body made up of three spheres of snow.

politically correct

◻ ◻ ◻

Again and again one finds the patterns that are discussed above (and elsewhere in these pages) repeated. Attacks on political correctness feature ludicrously awkward words with -*person* suffixes, advanced as if they were representative of what gender-neutral language is all about; assertions masquerading as arguments; and repeated suggestions that those advocating inclusive practices are trying to have those practices made mandatory—imposed by force on an unwilling population. One finds all too frequently as well a cherry picking of examples so as to suggest that, for example, academic policies requiring trigger warnings[1] are the norm at American universities--when the reality is that a tiny minority of institutions have even discussed any proposal that such a requirement be instituted.

As the above suggests, the vast majority of the attacks on "politically correct" language have come from conservative or reactionary commentators. But not all. Arguably the most interesting exception is an article David Foster Wallace wrote for *Harper's Magazine* in 2001. At the heart of his argument are these contentions:

> Usage is always political, of course, but it's complexly political. With respect, for instance, to political change, usage conventions can function in two ways. On the one hand, they can be a reflection of political change, and on the other hand

---

1   The fuss in recent years over this practice seems to the authors of this book to have been completely overblown. For a sane defense of the "considerate and reasonable practice" of giving a "heads up" to students in advance of teaching sensitive material, see Kate Manne, "Why I Use Trigger Warnings," *The New York Times*, 19 September 2015.

they can be an instrument of political change. These two functions are different and have to be kept straight. Confusing them—in particular, mistaking for political efficacy what is really just a language's political symbolism—enables the bizarre conviction that America ceases to be elitist or unfair because Americans stop using certain vocabulary that is historically associated with elitism and unfairness. This is PCE's [politically correct English's] central fallacy—that a society's mode of expression is productive of its attitudes rather than a product of those attitudes....[1]

Given that Wallace begins by acknowledging that language can work in two directions so far as politics is concerned, the accusation he makes regarding politically correct English is distinctly odd. There is surely no serious writer on this issue who claims that America or any other country will cease to be elitist or unfair simply by changing the language it uses. Those who advocated using *doctor* rather than *lady doctor* and *nurse* rather than *male nurse* did not do so in the belief that such linguistic change would be sufficient to change society's sexism regarding the profession of medicine. They did so in the awareness that pressing for linguistic change can be *an* instrument of political change—not the sole instrument, but one of many instruments that can help to bring political change. In alleging that the supporters of linguistic change believe that a society's mode of expression is productive of its attitudes *rather than* a product of those attitudes, Wallace frames the issue as a simple binary. In fact,

---

1   David Foster Wallace, "Tense Present: Democracy, English, and the Wars over Usage," *Harper's Magazine*, April 2001.

the fallacy is to assume that it need be *either/or*. Research has shown conclusively—as Wallace himself acknowledges at the beginning of this passage—that changes in language *both* reflect broader change *and* can help to bring about that change. Of course it's not possible to eliminate elitism and unfairness simply by ceasing to use "vocabulary that is historically associated with elitism and unfairness." But equally clear is that the perpetuation of such vocabulary can only help to perpetuate elitism and unfairness. Precisely how much difference language makes may be in dispute, but there is absolutely no question that it does make a difference.

Is that to say that political correctness as it is seen by critics is always a figment of the right-wing imagination, that it should never be a cause for concern? No, it's not. Much as the term may be abused, criticisms of the "politically correct" do sometimes strike a nerve. Much as conservatives dominate massively in business circles, in business-sponsored think-tanks, on talk radio, and in many, many other areas of North American life, there can be no question that one area—humanities and social sciences faculties of North American universities—is dominated by progressives, and that in those environs a measure of intolerance for conservative viewpoints is sometimes displayed. Right-wing commentators—themselves often entirely intolerant of opposing views—frequently exaggerate to a wild degree both the breadth and the depth of the intolerance that is sometimes to be found in humanities and social sciences faculties. But those of us who identify as progressives should not pretend it is an entirely imaginary phenomenon.

A reluctance to open up certain subjects for discussion for reasons of "political correctness" can also be found here and there outside of any academic environment. An interesting case in point is how gingerly progressives in the city of Van-couver have approached the issue of real estate prices in recent years. Vancouver real estate prices—always high—began to move into the stratosphere in the early 2010s. Not entirely by coincidence, the same half-decade was one in which changes within China led many fabulously wealthy people to look for "bankable" investments abroad. Investing in real estate in some of the world's most attractive and high real-estate value cities—London, New York, and a number of others as well as Vancouver—was for many far preferable to other investments. Nothing objectionable about that—or at least, nothing that should be any more the subject of com-plaint than the behavior of many of the very rich the world over for a very, very long time. But for many Vancouverites of modest means who didn't already own property themselves, the effect was crippling. With the average income of the city stuck around $50,000 in 2016, the average 2015 price of a detached home soared to $1,830,000. Many sounded the alarm: The city was becoming completely unaffordable for the average person; surely the situation was untenable. Man-dating greater density might go some distance towards mak-ing the city more affordable, but surely consideration should be given as well to changing zoning requirements such that less land would be devoted to luxury housing; to imposing taxes on foreign ownership (of the sort that numerous other cities worldwide impose); and to imposing taxes on non-resident owners (whether foreign or domestic). Regardless of the causes of the explosion in prices, such changes would surely help to make things more affordable for the average Vancouverite. But Vancouver Mayor Gregor Robertson and his fellow progressives for many years treaded cautiously, returning repeatedly to the theme that the situation should

politically correct

not be interpreted as being "about race" in a highly multi-racial city. They have paid lip service to the importance of doing something about affordability—but until late 2016 they did little or nothing to address the issue. Those calling for action made clear again and again that they saw the issue as being rich buyers from afar crowding out local people of modest means, and that it had nothing to do with the nationality or racial or cultural background of those buyers. For years, it made no difference.

Now it may be fairly pointed out that politicians have reasons other than "political correctness" for hesitating to do anything that might have the effect of bringing down the house prices of their constituents; home owners vote at higher rates than renters, and the rich vote at higher rates than the poor. And it's fair too to be concerned about the possibility of inflaming racial feeling. But it also seems fair to suggest the possibility that (as Jonathan Kay has put it in the left-of-center magazine *The Walrus*) "a narrow fixation on identity politics has compromised the left's traditional focus on wide-angle issues of socio-economic stratification, poverty, and income inequality." In its anxiety not to make the issue "about race," is the city not doing enough about making housing affordable for the poor—or, indeed, the middle class? In Kay's view, "as homes become unaffordable; political correctness is polarizing the left."[1]

More generally, it's worth noting that, much as "politically correct" may have begun as a term that related very largely to one's attitude to economic issues—and to capitalism and socialism in general—it's come to be applied more and more to cultural concerns, and less and less to economic or class ones.

---

1   Jonathan Kay, "Vancouver's Offshore Problem," *The Walrus*, May 2016.

This tendency may well account for a good deal of what animates David Foster Wallace's hostility toward "politically correct English." Tellingly, the examples he uses are more often about poverty and social class than they are about gender, race, or sexual orientation:

> Were I, for instance, a political conservative who opposed taxation as a means of redistributing national wealth, I would be delighted to watch PCE progressives spend their time and energy arguing over whether a poor person should be described as "low income" or as "economically challenged" or "pre-prosperous" rather than constructing effective public arguments for redistributive legislation or for higher marginal tax rates on corporations....
>
> As a practical matter, I strongly doubt whether a guy who has four small kids and makes $12,000 a year feels more empowered or less ill-used by a society that carefully refers to him as "economically disadvantaged" rather than "poor." Were I he, in fact, I'd probably find the PCE term insulting—not just because it's patronizing but because it's hypocritical and self-serving.... PCE functions primarily to signal, and congratulate certain virtues in the speaker—scrupulous egalitarianism, concern for the dignity of all people, sophistication about the political implications of language— and so serves the selfish interests of the PC far more than it serves any of the persons or groups renamed.

politically correct

This is of course invective, and like far-right critics of "political correctness," Wallace often resorts to hyperbole and straw figures. It is preposterous to suggest that the terms *economically challenged* and *pre-prosperous* have gained credence among progressives as alternatives to *poor*. The term *low-income*, on the other hand, has indeed been put forward as an alternative—and not only by those in some PC ivory tower; it's been adopted by many who really do have very little money. According to the Google counter, "My family is low-income" appears more than 52,000 times—more than half as often as "My family is poor," which appears 95,000 times. No doubt there are some like Wallace's hypothetical "guy who has four small kids," but clearly a lot of poor people are quite comfortable referring to themselves as *low-income*. Is it obvious that *low-income* is preferable to *poor*? No. But is it also not obvious that *poor*—which has so many associations beyond the economic—is preferable to *low-income*.

Nor is it obvious that the typical person who uses terms such as *low-income* is a hypocritical, self-serving elitist who cares only about the niceties of language and does nothing to actually help those who need it. Here again Wallace is peddling false dichotomies. It's not an *either/or*; there is no reason whatsoever that people in positions of privilege can't consider the question of what is or is not appropriate language *and* also do their best to construct effective public arguments for redistributive legislation or for higher marginal tax rates on corporations. (Or, for that matter, pitch in at the local food bank or homeless shelter or anti-poverty office.)

When its logic is analyzed, then, Wallace's case simply falls apart. But the logic of an argument is not everything.

Does Wallace's caricature come close to describing a real type among progressives? Does he touch a nerve?

Yes and no. Our sense is that the caricature for the most part misses the mark—but not because there aren't at least a few hypocritical, self-serving elitists in progressive circles. Of course there are, just as there are more than a few hypocritical, self-serving elitists among conservatives, among evangelical Christians, among military officers—among just about any group you can name. Where Wallace perhaps touches a nerve is in the suggestion that, on the whole, people who are concerned about inclusive language haven't done as much as they might have to help the poor. On the whole that's probably true. But neither have they spent a lot of time in the ways that he suggests, worrying about what words should be used to describe people in poverty; our sense is that most progressives have spent relatively little time on these issues—either on the saying or the doing. When it comes to gays and lesbians, progressives have pushed *both* for more inclusive language when we talk about gays and lesbians *and* for a wide variety of legislative and legal changes regarding gays and lesbians. When it comes to gender, progressives have pushed *both* for more gender-neutral language *and* for legislative and legal changes affecting women; when it comes to racial and cultural differences, progressives have pushed *both* for linguistic changes when we talk about racial and cultural groups *and* for legislative and legal changes affecting those groups. In comparison to those areas, progressives have spent relatively little time on issues such as how best to speak of *rich* and *poor* (or of *making good money, earning a good income, coming from a good family, high net worth*—the list goes on, as we discuss elsewhere in these pages). Nor have those on the left spent as much time in recent generations as the left did in the early and mid-twentieth century pushing for legislative and legal changes that would materially improve the lot of those in poverty. From the 1930s through to the early 1970s there was much talk of waging war on poverty—and much action taken too. Compare that to recent decades: in election after election, candidates are allowed to focus virtually all their attention on what they would do for the middle class—never saying what they would do for those whose affiliation with the middle class is no more than aspirational. The recent drive for higher minimum wages has for the most part come not from progressive academics or politicians, but from the low-paid workers themselves. Even when middle-class progressives focus on inequality, the reference points are usually comparisons not between absurdly overpaid CEOs and the lowest-paid worker, but between absurdly overpaid CEOs and the median worker;[1] again, the focus is more on the struggles of the middle class than on those of people in poverty.

So far as language goes, the amount of time and effort we devote to how we should speak of the poor is dwarfed by the amount of time we spend on developing gender-neutral terminology, appropriate inclusive terminology for those of varying sexual orientations, those of varying levels of ability or disability, and so on. And so far as results are concerned, the outlook for women, for gays and lesbians, for the disabled, and for various other groups has improved markedly over the past couple of generations (in North America at least),

---

1   See for example Jenny Che, "Here's How Outrageous the Pay Gap between CEOs and Workers Is," *The Huffington Post*, 28 August 2015; and Roberto A. Ferdman, "The Pay Gap between CEOs and Workers Is Much Worse Than You Realize," *The Washington Post*, 25 September 2014.

whereas the outlook for low-income people has worsened. That's no reason for any of us to pay less attention than has been paid to issues of gender, or race, or sexual orientation, or disability. But it's reason for those of us who care about both language and social justice to pay more attention to the way we speak of poor people—and to what we are doing materially to improve the circumstances of poor people. In both categories, the authors of this book would argue, what we've been doing is not enough.

Whatever their shortcomings, Wallace's criticisms offer a refreshing difference from right-wing attacks on inclusive language, not least of all in that they do not pretend that such language is being forced down our throats by some imaginary thought-and-language police. That is perhaps the single most egregious respect in which the charges against progressives by the far-right have typically been exaggerated or (for want of a better term) trumped up. In America or Canada or Britain or Brazil or South Africa, no one is in danger of being sent to prison for saying *that's so gay*, and no media outlets are in danger of being shut down for writing of *man* rather than *humanity*.

That's not the case in certain other parts of the world. It's worth remembering when we speak of "political correctness" that in some countries its strictures are as real as they were in Joseph Stalin's Soviet Union in the 1930s. In Xi Zinping's China, failing to adhere to the "correct political orientation" is increasingly likely to bring grave consequences; those who do not follow "correct guidance" in what they write about political, economic and cultural matters are subject to censorship, loss of employment, or imprisonment.[1] In India the RSS, a Hindu nationalist group that scorns as "politically correct" those who would make India a more open and inclusive society for non-Hindus (and for "low-caste" Hindus, and for women, and for gays and lesbians), has come to exert great influence over the media, as well as over the content of school textbooks. And of course similar strictures continue to prevail in authoritarian regimes around the world, from Belarus to Zimbabwe to North Korea.

It's worth remembering too that those living in jurisdictions where the cries against "political correctness" are loudest may also be subject to genuinely serious restrictions on freedom of speech (albeit restrictions that are less severe and less widespread than those in countries such as China or Zimbabwe or Belarus). Real impositions, real censorship. But in America these are not restrictions imposed by "politically correct" progressives. Several American states, for example, now have "ag-gag" laws on their books, making "interference with agricultural production"—defined as bringing to the attention of the public what actually happens behind the closed doors of factory farms—a criminal offence. In Idaho you can go to jail for making a video that reveals to the public the reality of hideous cruelty to our fellow creatures that constitutes the modern farm.

Finally, it's worth remembering that, so far as language is concerned, pressure for change comes as much from the political right as it does from the left. No one condemns it as "politically correct" when right-wingers strive to give the term *free enterprise* wider currency than the term

---

1   See Andrew J. Nathan, "Who Is Xi?," *New York Review of Books*, 12 May 2016, and David Bandurski, "Mirror, Mirror on the Wall," *China Media Project*, 20 February 2016.

capitalism, or the term *pro-life* wider currency than the term *anti-abortion*, or the term *enhanced interrogation methods* wider currency than *torture*, or the terms *intensive farming* and *conventional farming methods* wider currency than the term *factory farming*. Nor is it condemned as "politically correct" when conservatives endeavor to frame the argument against gun control as *protecting Second Amendment rights*.

Is it worth trying to formulate a pejorative general term for these efforts by right-wingers to reshape the language? No—in our view another overarching concept of that sort would serve little purpose. Interesting though their history may be, overarching concepts such as political correctness are, in our view, of limited usefulness in any honest effort to confront the challenges of how best to use language in ways that contribute to making the world a better place.

No doubt the language we use—what we say—will never be as important as what we do. But language is not unimportant; saying can be a form of doing, and language can play an important role in helping us to do the right thing. To treat men and women on an equal footing, to avoid discrimination on the basis of religion, or class, or race, or sexual orientation—language can be used to help accomplish all these goals, and more. But the effort to do so requires attention to the details; each case in point deserves to be thought through—and, in many cases, argued through. This book is dedicated to making that effort.

politically correct

Postscript: 2017

The text of most of this book was written before the extraordinary events of the presidential campaign of 2016; the following postscript is prompted in large part by those events.

In the past year or two the process of broadening the concept of political correctness seems to have accelerated. In some workplaces, for example, "politically correct" has become synonymous not with any set of attitudes towards ethical and political issues outside the office, but with an excessive sensitivity towards the way in which powerful people within the organization might react to a proposal to do things differently; if one is too careful to follow the organization's long-accepted ways of doing things, one's approach may sometimes be labeled too politically correct. And in the realm of politics, Donald Trump has done a great deal to broaden the ways in which the term *political correctness* is applied. One way in which he has used the term seems to equate with what most people would ordinarily call simple politeness, or tact, or decency. If, for example, you have known someone for a long time and been friends, but you become at some point rivals for a coveted position and start to feel some animosity towards that person, should you do your best to put a lid on any feelings of animosity and emphasize the positive in what you say about your rival—or should you be "honest" about showing every bit of animosity to the world? In Trump's view, you should let the hate show through; anything else is "politicians' speak" or "politically correct crap" that is in itself worthy of hate:

> This is what bothers me about politicians....
> [Marco Rubio] announces he's gonna run [for

President] and [reporters] go to [rival Presidential candidate] Jeb Bush, and ask "what do you think of Marco Rubio?" "He's my dear, dear friend, he's wonderful, he's a wonderful person, I'm so happy that he's running."

Give me a break. That's called politicians' speak.

Then they go to Marco [and they ask] "what do you think of Jeb Bush?" "Oh, he's great, he's brought me along, he's wonderful." They hate each other, but they can't say it. They hate each other. It really does bother me when I see [Rubio's people], and I see Jeb, and maybe that's what you want, and maybe that's the kind of people that are going to get elected. Maybe [people] don't want a straight talker, maybe they don't. But I am so tired of this politically correct crap.[1]

politically correct

It wasn't just politeness and civility that Republican candidates in the 2016 presidential race tried to throw into disrepute with their attacks on political correctness. The campaign took ideas of what constituted "political correctness" in several even more extraordinary directions, with several candidates suggesting that it was the single biggest thing wrong with America. As Karen Tumulty and Jenna Johnson of *The Washington Post* summed it up, political correctness was, for Republicans, "the all-purpose enemy," with the candidates suggesting it as "the explanation for seemingly every threat [confronting] the country: terrorism, illegal immigration, an economic recovery that is leaving many behind, to name just a few."[2]

---

1   Donald Trump, "I'm So Tired of This Politically Correct Crap," video on *Politico*, 22 September 2015.
2   Karen Tumulty and Jenna Johnson, "Why Trump May Be Winning the War

"Political correctness is killing people," argued Republican Senator Ted Cruz; "Political correctness is ruining our country," chimed in fellow Republican Ben Carson. Famously, they were joined by Trump, whose view of how widely the dangers of political correctness might extend was even broader. Trump, for example, responded to the targeted anti-gay, anti-Hispanic violence that occurred in Orlando in June, 2016 in part by blaming "political correctness":

> If we do not get tough and smart real fast, we are not going to have a country anymore. Because our leaders are weak, I said this was going to happen—and it is only going to get worse. I am trying to save lives and prevent the next terrorist attack. We can't afford to be politically correct anymore.[1]

Trump has often been quoted as saying that "the big problem this country has is [being] politically correct," but the full context of that quotation is often not provided. It deserves to be. The occasion was a debate during the presidential primary season among Republican candidates for President. Megyn Kelly of Fox News was the moderator.

> **Kelly**: You've called women you don't like "fat pigs," [audience laughter] "dogs," [more audience laughter] "slobs" and "disgusting animals" …
>
> **Trump**: Only Rosie O'Donnell. [applause and prolonged laughter from the audience[2]]

---

on Political Correctness," *The Washington Post*, 4 January 2016.

1   Donald Trump, "Statement Regarding the Tragic Terrorist Attack in Orlando, Florida," 12 June 2016.

2   It is interesting to watch the video footage closely; although the applause and laughter are loud, it appears from the video that no more than perhaps a third of the (all-Republican) crowd is laughing and applauding.

Kelly: No, it wasn't. For the record, it was well beyond Rosie O'Donnell.

Trump: I'm sure it was.

Kelly: Your Twitter account has several disparaging comments about women's looks. You once told a contestant on "Celebrity Apprentice" it would be a "pretty picture" to see her on her knees. Does that sound to you like the temperament of a man we should elect as president? And how will you answer the charge … that you are part of the war on women?

Trump: I think the big problem this country has is [being] politically correct. I've been challenged by so many people and I don't frankly have the time for total political correctness. And to be honest with you, this country doesn't have time either. This country is in big trouble. We don't win anymore. We lose to China, we lose to Mexico both in trade and at the border. We lose to everybody. Frankly what I say—and oftentimes it's fun, it's kidding, we have a good time…. But you know what? We, we need strength, we need energy, we need quickness and we need brain in this country to turn it around. That I can tell you right now.[1]

In other words, it constitutes "total political correctness" to object to slurs such as "'fat pigs,' 'dogs,' 'slobs' and 'disgusting animals'"—and it's that sort of political correctness that's a

---

1   "Donald Trump to Megyn Kelly: I Don't Have Time for Political Correctness and Neither Does This Country," video of 6 August 2015 Republican Presidential Candidates Debate, *Real Clear Politics*. The notes in square brackets as to applause and laughter have been added by the authors of this book.

big part of the problem with America—not the slurs themselves. In Trump's view, demeaning remarks about women are all in good fun, and fussing about words is an unnecessary distraction when there are a lot more important things we should be paying attention to.

It may well be that Trump's equation of the supposed excesses of political correctness with what to most of us seems like common decency has inflated the notion of political correctness so extravagantly that the whole balloon will burst and be no more. If so, that would, in the opinion of this book's authors, be no bad thing; it can often be far more fruitful to think through individual issues to do with language and ethics and politics on their own terms rather than trying to conceptualize each issue in terms of any overarching category—even when it's a category that *hasn't* been tainted by dubious assumptions and abusive language. Standards of decency might be well served if we give the concept of political correctness a rest.

Crude and irresponsible attacks on so-called political correctness by people such as President Trump are one thing. But what of the genuine doubts of decent people who are resistant to change—who on issues of this sort instinctively lean towards the views of Edmund Burke: "it were better you were less new-fangled in your speech, for the sake of grammar"?[1] The authors of this book agree that, on many specific issues, the Burkean view has considerable merit. We should resist the use of *disinterested* to mean *uninterested*; that is change that represents loss with no corresponding gain. We should resist the loss of linguistic precision that the wearing away of the past perfect tense brings with it.

---

1   *Letters on a Regicide Peace: Fourth Letter to the Earl Fitzwilliam on the Proposals for Peace with the Regicide Directory of France*, 1795.

And there are many more examples. But it will also be evident that on many specific issues the authors of this book endorse change. What have we to say by way of reassurance to the teacher who has always put a red mark beside "they" in a sentence such as "Everybody opened the presents they had been given," when *The Washington Post* and many other authorities now say "they" is quite acceptable in such contexts? What have we to say to the farm child who has grown up calling a sow or a boar an *it*—when it's now suggested to him that farm animals be called *he* or *she*? Or to the student who is uneasy at the prospect of a fellow student asking to be referred to in the third person as *them* instead of as *him*?

To some extent reassurance may be found in the past. It's to be found in the history of writers such as William Shakespeare and Jane Austen having used "the singular they" with words such as *everyone* and *anyone*; it's to be found in the history of *he* and *she* being used widely to denote farm animals before the onset of factory farming; it's to be found in previous changes in pronoun use—such as the shift through which *you* came to replace *thou* and *thee* as the subject and object pronouns we use to address another person.

But of course not all changes have parallels in the past or entail a return to past usages; we advocate many changes out of arguments from first principles, and most of those changes do not have centuries of specific historical precedents to back them up. That is not to say, however, that they are without precedent altogether. The history of language itself is a history of change, and much of that change has been based on changes in our ways of thinking about ethical and political issues. Among the most notable changes in language over the past two hundred years are those that have occurred in connection with changing attitudes towards

politically correct

gender and race: women and people of color have finally begun to be treated—and spoken of—on the basis of principles of equality. And over the past half century our ways of speaking—like our laws—have begun to treat anyone whose sexual orientation is same-sex with the same rights and the same respect that heterosexual humans are accorded. The word *gay* is these days hardly ever used in its old sense, but in that sense it has many possible substitutes, whereas the language was sorely in need of a non-pejorative substitute for *homosexual* and its even more pejorative synonyms. Such change has not been accomplished because people thought of *being good* only in terms of what was universally accepted in that era. They thought too of how to do *better*, of how to make the world a better place. We should never let that impulse die within us.

BIAS-FREE VOCABULARY: A SHORT LIST

actress . . . . actor

admitted or
    avowed homosexual . . . . . . openly gay person

alderman . . . . councilor

anchorman . . . . anchor/news anchor

Asiatic . . . . Asian

bad guy . . . . villain

bellboy . . . . bellhop

bogeyman . . . . bogey monster

brotherhood . . . . fellowship, community
*(Note: Brotherhood is of course perfectly acceptable for
describing all-male situations.)*

businessman . . . . businessperson,
                                entrepreneur

caveman . . . . cave-dweller

chairman . . . . chair

cleaning lady . . . . cleaner

clergyman . . . . minister,
                                member of the clergy

common man . . . . common person, average
                                person, ordinary person

congressman . . . . representative

con-man . . . . con-artist

craftsman . . . . craftsperson, artisan

draftsman . . . . drafter

Eskimo. . . . . Inuit
(Note: This only applies in Canada; in Alaska, Eskimo is commonly used and is not considered offensive.)

farmer's wife . . . . farmer

fireman . . . . firefighter

fisherman . . . . fisher

forefathers. . . . . ancestors

foreman. . . . . manager, supervisor

freshman . . . . first-year student

frontman . . . . figurehead, front

garbageman. . . . . garbage collector

grandfather . . . . grandparent
(Note: As in "Those currently covered by the old provisions will be grandfathered in.")

gunman . . . . shooter

gyp. . . . . cheat, con

Gypsies . . . . Roma
(Note: When a nomadic people from India began to appear in Britain in the late medieval period, they were thought to have come from Egypt and were termed 'gypcian. Over the centuries, however, Gypsies was very frequently used in a derogatory way; the term Roma has now come to be generally accepted as the best term for those outside the culture to use. Gypsy may still be a useful term of self-description for some of Roma background.)

handyman . . . . handyperson

hearing impaired . . . . deaf, Deaf, or hard
                                              of hearing
(Note: This depends on context; in limited contexts, hearing impaired may be appropriate.)

homosexual couple. . . . . couple, gay couple
(if sexual orientation is
relevant)

homosexual marriage . . . . . . same-sex marriage,
gay marriage

Indian. . . . . Aboriginal, First Nations,
First Peoples (in Canada),
American Indian, Native
American (in the United
States)

*(Note: The key consideration here is sensitivity to audience.
If you do not belong to the group but you know that the
people you are writing about prefer a particular designation,
that is the one to use.)*

infantryman. . . . . footsoldier

insurance man. . . . . insurance agent

layman . . . . layperson

longshoreman . . . . shiploader, stevedore

maid. housekeeper

mailman. . . . . letter carrier, mail carrier

male nurse. . . . . nurse

man . . . . humanity

man (an exhibit) . . . . staff

man (a barricade) . . . . fortify, occupy

man (a ship). . . . . crew

man enough. . . . . strong enough

man hours. . . . . staff time, work hours

man of letters . . . . person of letters,
intellectual

bias-free vocabulary

manhandle	rough-up, maul
manhole	sewer hole, access hole
manhole cover	sewer cover
mankind	humankind, people, humanity, humans
manly	self-confident, courageous, straightforward
manmade	handmade, human-made, constructed
manned spaceflight	crewed spaceflight, human spaceflight
mentally retarded person	person with an intellectual disability
middleman	intermediary, go-between
midget	little person, dwarf, person of short stature
minority group	marginalized group
mother tongue	native language
mothering	parenting
negro	black, Black, African American
niggardly	stingy

(Note: The word niggardly has no etymological connection with nigger. Since the one suggests the other to many minds, however, it is safer to avoid using it.)

non-transgender	cisgender
non-white people	people of color, racialized people

Oriental. . . . . Asian, Middle Eastern

penmanship. . . . . handwriting

policeman . . . . police officer

postman . . . . letter carrier, mail carrier

Renaissance man. . . . . Renaissance person,
polymath

salesman, saleslady . . . . salesperson, sales clerk,
sales representative

sex change operation . . . . sex reassignment surgery,
gender confirmation
surgery

Siamese twins . . . . conjoined twins

snowman. . . . . snowbody (rhymes with
nobody)

spokesman . . . . representative,
spokesperson, agent

sportsman. . . . . sportsperson

stewardess . . . . flight attendant

straw man . . . . straw figure, straw dog

thinking man . . . . intellectual, thinking
person

transgendered. . . . . transgender

unsportsmanlike . . . . unsporting

waitress. . . . . server

weatherman . . . . weather forecaster

womanly . . . . warm, tender, nurturing,
sympathetic

workman. . . . . worker, laborer

bias-free vocabulary

INDEX

index

index

From the Publisher

A name never says it all, but the word "Broadview" expresses a good deal of the philosophy behind our company. We are open to a broad range of academic approaches and political viewpoints. We pay attention to the broad impact book publishing and book printing has in the wider world; we began using recycled stock more than a decade ago, and for some years now we have used 100% recycled paper for most titles. Our publishing program is internationally oriented and broad-ranging. Our individual titles often appeal to a broad readership too; many are of interest as much to general readers as to academics and students.

Founded in 1985, Broadview remains a fully independent company owned by its shareholders—not an imprint or subsidiary of a larger multinational.

For the most accurate information on our books (including information on pricing, editions, and formats) please visit our website at www.broadviewpress.com. Our print books and ebooks are also available for sale on our site.

On the Broadview website we also offer several goods that are not books—among them the Broadview coffee mug, the Broadview beer stein (inscribed with a line from Geoffrey Chaucer's *Canterbury Tales*), the Broadview fridge magnets (your choice of philosophical or literary), and a range of T-shirts (made from combinations of hemp, bamboo, and/or high-quality pima cotton, with no child labor, sweatshop labor, or environmental degradation involved in their manufacture).

All these goods are available through the "merchandise" section of the Broadview website. When you buy Broadview goods you can support other goods too.

broadview press   ·
www.broadviewpress.com

The interior of this book is printed on 100% recycled paper.